Viva El Becks

Viva El Becks

An Intimate portrait of the world's favourite football star

Photographs by
Ramon Perez Sanroman and
Rolando Cardeñoso Benito

Solarpix

Words by
Gerard Couzens

JOHN BLAKE

Published by John Blake Publishing Ltd,
3, Bramber Court, 2 Bramber Road,
London W14 9PB, England

www.blake.co.uk

First published in hardback in 2005

ISBN 1 84454 185 1

British Library Cataloguing-in-Publication Data:

A catalogue record for this book is available from
the British Library.

Design by www.envydesign.co.uk

Printed in Spain by Bookprint S.L.

1 3 5 7 9 10 8 6 4 2

Papers used by John Blake Publishing are natural,
recyclable products made from wood grown in
sustainable forests. The manufacturing processes
conform to the environmental regulations of the
country of origin.

Acknowledgements

We would like to thank the following photographers and agencies for contributing additional images which allowed us to complete *Viva El Becks*:

Darren Fletcher
Eduardo Brilliones
Luis Sevillano
Warren Johnson
David Toms
Marca Media
Prisma
Europa Press
Michelle Chaplow
Mirrorpix
Mata-Sayago

In addition we would like to acknowledge the following for allowing us to reproduce past articles from their publication within the book:

Daily Express
Daily Mirror
Heat Magazine
New Magazine
Star Magazine
The *Sun*

Special thanks to Len Greener, Rob Greener and Blaze Communication for their continuing support.

Richard Atkins and Mark Beltran
Solarpix Photo agency directors

Contents

Introduction

The day Manchester United announced they were selling David Beckham to Real Madrid marked a new era for the England captain and his fans. Becks had grown from boy to man with the club he joined as a 16-year-old trainee, manager Alex Ferguson had become like a father to him and the city of Manchester had adopted the lad from Essex as one of their own. Millions of admirers, from the Far East to South America, were used to switching on their TV sets to see him in the red and white of the only Premiership team he had ever played for. Home was Beckingham Palace in Hertfordshire or millionaires' row at Alderley Edge in Cheshire, he did his shopping at Marks & Spencer and his favourite food was Super Noodles.

On 18 June 2003 – the day Manchester United announced to the Stock Exchange they were selling David to Real Madrid for £24.5 million – all that changed. England lost its number-one soccer and media icon to a foreign giant. And former Spice Girl Victoria Beckham, the other half of the golden couple dubbed the New Royals, put one foot in Madrid in response to her husband's move.

Viva El Becks looks in words and pictures at David's Spanish experience. It recalls the first frenzied months of his life in Madrid as his hero's welcome gave way to problems with the press and the exasperation of finding a new home. It relives the shocking moments as David's image as the perfect husband and father crumbled under allegations he had

cheated on Victoria with a string of beautiful women, including former PR Rebecca Loos.

It examines the Beckhams' fight back, Victoria's decision to move to Madrid full-time and the birth of her third son Cruz against a background of constant rumours she missed England and, given the choice, would have boarded the first plane out of Spain. And it looks at David's efforts on the pitch to forget the distractions of his private life and persuade Real Madrid fans he is more than a media-made superstar.

The book comes with the stamp of authority of the journalists who have witnessed it all – including the photographers who have followed Beckham every step of the way and

whose images now help to chart this fascinating period in the life of one of the world's most famous faces.

Hola, Becks!

Even for a soccer superstar like David Beckham, it was one hell of an entrance. Real Madrid's new *galactico* was brought to the Spanish capital for his medical courtesy of a private Gulfstream jet, a chauffeur-driven saloon car … and a police escort.

It was an arrival fit for a king. Four police motorcyclists with guns in their hip-holsters and sunglasses over their eyes flanked Beckham's Audi A8 as it screeched into the grounds of the privately owned Clinica Zarzuela. Half a dozen bodyguards rode in front in a Lexus four-wheel drive. Patients and medical staff hung from balconies on the four-storey building on the outskirts of Madrid, trying to take pictures as keepsakes. More than a hundred fans screamed the

England captain's name as he stepped out in a pair of blue jeans split at the knee and a brilliant-white jacket over a white shirt. And twice that number of newsmen and photographers from around the world added to the decibels by shouting questions from behind barricades around the hospital entrance as Becks briefly posed for pictures on the clinic steps.

The satellite-news trucks had started arriving just after breakfast – around the same time Beckham was buckling his seat belt for the two-and-a-half-hour flight to Madrid. Outpatients arriving for check-ups found themselves caught up in the lead story of the day as journalists thrust business cards into their hands and asked them to try and find out what was going on inside. Passers-by swelled

An arrival fit for a king – David and Victoria make their entrance.

the crowds drawn by the cameras as the morning wore on. All these surreal scenes were relayed live to Spanish TV by news crews chasing Beckham by motorbike from the VIP airstrip where he touched down at two minutes past midday local time.

The waiting that preceded those days of Beckham-mania in Madrid, as the city counted down the hours to his arrival, came to an end on 1 July 2003. For months Beckham's future had been the source of intense media speculation as his relationship with Manchester United manager Alex Ferguson soured.

The transfer saga that ended with David's move to Madrid captured the world's attention. Barcelona seemed to have stolen the initiative over their Spanish rivals and Italian sides AC Milan and Inter by agreeing a deal with Manchester United while the England captain was on holiday in America in the summer of 2003. New Barcelona president Joan Laporta based his whole presidential campaign on his promise to bring the world's most high-profile footballer to the Nou Camp. What neither Manchester nor Barcelona had counted on was Beckham's steely reserve to play for what he saw as the best club in the world. Real Madrid took

Becks surveying the crowds from his balcony at the Santo Mauro Hotel, where the couple stayed on their arrival in the city.

the rare step of issuing a statement denying they had any interest in signing David at the end of April 2003.

'Never, never, never. Nobody at Real has ever spoken about Beckham and I don't want to start now,' said club president Florentino Perez.

'We are very happy with our current team and will never, ever sign Beckham.'

The wind must have taken his words because less than two months later Manchester United were confirming they had agreed to sell David to the Spanish giants. The news broke as Posh and Becks flew to Japan to capitalise on their star status with a promotional tour.

As Beckham walked through the doors of the Clinica Zarzuela, the only hurdle separating the boy from Essex and a £90,000-a-week four-year contract was a 90-minute medical. Real Madrid obviously didn't harbour any doubts he'd sail through. A cameraman recorded Beckham's efforts to impress their medics for their in-house TV channel. Excerpts were subsequently sold to stations

The Santiago Bernabeu Stadium, Real's home ground.

around the world. And when the club's Chief Medical Officer, Alfonso del Corral, confirmed Beckham had passed and was 'as fit as a bull', the scene was set for the star's presentation as a Real Madrid player.

Beckham signed his new contract with a ballpoint pen wife Victoria had given him as a present. Before putting pen to paper on the deal, he managed to fit in a kick-around with son Brooklyn at Real Madrid's Santiago Bernabeu stadium. Afterwards he headed back to his private £1,300-a-night suite at the five-star Gran Melia Fenix Hotel – the same hotel the Beatles picked in 1965 when they played Madrid – to spend the evening with his family. It was his first and only chance to put his feet up during one of the most closely scrutinised football signings of all time.

Even then, it didn't take long for word to get around about where Beckham was staying and for his new army of fans to start massing at the doors of the hotel next to Madrid's Hard Rock Café, in the hope of an autograph. Groups of girls gave the hotel doormen an afternoon to remember by pressing up against the glass in the revolving doors in the hope of catching a glimpse of the footballer. Others waited in cars in a side road with the engine running – ready to give chase along with the photographers at the slightest sign of any movement.

Once it was confirmed he was on his way to Madrid, the speculation about Beckham's future gave way to speculation about his shirt number. At Manchester United Becks was number seven. The number seven at Real Madrid was already worn by fans' favourite Raul and it seemed improbable a man of even David's star status would try and claim it for himself. Beckham was offered the number four of former defender Fernando Hierro and the number twenty- three, which was also available.

Once again, Posh is said to have played a determining role in the life of her husband by telling him twenty-three was the number of basketball legend Michael Jordan and encouraging him to pick it. Cynics saw the commercial hand of Real Madrid behind the choice – a number that would appeal to Americans and help it fly off the shelves in the US. It prompted Internet debates about underlying mystical meanings – we have twenty-three pairs of chromosomes, Julius Caesar was stabbed twenty-three times, 23mph is the maximum speed of an American crow. Whatever the real reason, the shirt would go on to become Real Madrid's best seller ever. After they went on sale at 1pm on 2 July, the club shop at the Santiago Bernabeu sold 200 of the £60 shirts in the first hour alone. Entire families queued up to get their hands on

Unable to have his familiar number 7 shirt at Real, Becks chose 23 – he even personalised his Lamborghini wheels with the number, in the same colour and style as his shirt.

Like father, like son. Real fans were pleased to see Brooklyn sporting a replica of dad's shirt.

the jersey. And British newspapers sent reporters to buy sackfuls of the shirts in medium, large and extra large so they could organise raffles for their readers.

In the run-up to David's official presentation as a Real Madrid player, the Spanish sports press trawled up old photos showing former striker Michael Laudrup's presentation in 1994 in front of just twenty reporters and photographers. The Danish frontman was a true *galactico* of his time. But his presentation was small fry compared to the welcome the England captain received. A staggering 520 journalists were accredited from twenty-five countries for the Beckham show – more than that year's Oscars, a European Champions match or a Real Madrid– Barcelona derby.

Real Madrid had anticipated the huge demand and set aside their basketball stadium for the event. There wasn't a seat left in the house as footballing legend Alfredo di Stefano presented Becks with his new shirt at the Raimundo Saiporta basketball arena next to the soccer training ground. TV cameramen broadcast the event live to living rooms in Britain, Japan, France, the USA, Chile, Portugal and Germany. Journalists from countries as far afield as Mexico, Norway, Costa Rica, China, Colombia, Brazil and north Africa also attended.

President Florentino Perez had his

soundbites off to a tee, declaring as the ceremony started, 'David Beckham comes from the Theatre of Dreams and he comes to the team of his dreams.'

And there proved to be something for everyone in the stage-managed ceremony when a watching fan planted a white cat in Posh's arms as a present when she was leaving. Outside in the stands, overlooking the training pitch, around 1,000 fans had virtually gatecrashed their way in and were singing in rhyming Spanish, 'Beckham, Beckham, cojonudo, como Beckham no hay ninguno' – 'Beckham, Beckham, big balls, like Beckham there's no other.'

Becks's admirers included ten-year-old Vera Bianco Fernandez, who had bunked school and bodypainted 'Beck' on her left cheek and 'Ham' on her right. On her right arm she had scrawled, 'I love you Beckham' next to a heart and on her left, 'Beckham the best.'

But the true highlight of the day came when ten-year-old Alfonso Lopez Iniguez slipped under a wire fence, ran on to the pitch as David emerged to do keepy-uppies in front of the fans in his new strip, and literally threw himself into his hero's arms. He was upon the England captain before his bodyguards realised what was happening. But instead of shooing him away or letting security take him off, David responded by hugging him and dressing him in the world's first Real Madrid Beckham

replica shirt – albeit an adult-size shirt that reached his knees. It was the perfect PR moment – David Beckham, the family man, wowing fans on only his second day in town with a show of spontaneous affection towards an emotional schoolboy. Hearts melted, dozens of camera shutters clicked instantaneously, fans in the crowd broke into applause – Becks had come and conquered. He was flying back home with his idol ranking up a few notches.

Opposite, above and left: The shirt presentation attracted huge amounts of media and fan attention.

Below right: Posh watches as Becks receives his new number – it is rumoured she helped him choose between numbers 4 and 23.

Advantage Beckham.
The couple spotted at
the Madrid Masters
Tennis Competition.

Hotel life

Beckham-mania was still at fever pitch when the England captain returned to Spain from a short summer break in the south of France. It was 23 July 2003 and David was back for his new team's tour of the Far East. In those two days he spent in the Spanish capital before flying out to China with his teammates, David got a sharp taste of the goldfish-bowl lifestyle he would have to endure until he found a proper home.

The five-star Santo Mauro – the hotel that would become Beckham's pad for the next three months – also lost the anonymity afforded by its hideaway in a tree-lined residential street in central Madrid. Crowds of fans mingled with TV crews and paparazzi outside the hotel as soon as word got around that David was

there. The Santo Mauro was a nineteenth-century former palace and hotel of choice for Hollywood actress Gwyneth Paltrow when she was in town. Beckham's Hollywood friend Tom Cruise would also check in when he was visiting Madrid. Over the coming months he and his then girlfriend, Penelope Cruz, would stay at least twice. And two years on when Cruise promoted *War of the Worlds* in Madrid, he would stay in the same suite as Beckham had, with new girlfriend Katie Holmes.

For the press pack following Beckham, though, the hotel was then the daily pick-up point for the gruelling chases of the first few weeks. It was also the scene of frequent rows with traffic wardens, who seemed to have doubled

The five-star Santo Mauro hotel, where David spent the first months of his time in Madrid. Fans thought that his early drop in form was due to the fact he was living out of a suitcase.

The press pack in Spain pursued the new signing wherever he went.

in number overnight. Not that they had to worry about following him to a football match just yet. Beckham spent his first full day back in Madrid filming commercials – a Japanese TV ad for chocolates in the morning and a clothes ad in the afternoon. In what was to be the start of Becks's tortured relationship with the press, a convoy of twenty cars carrying sports photographers, tabloid-style paparazzi and reporters followed him everywhere – jumping red lights and jockeying for positions behind him in a Princess Diana-style chase, desperate not to lose him.

They and hundreds of fans brought Madrid's Barajas Airport to a standstill the following day to see Beckham and his teammates off to China on the first leg of their Far East tour. Crowds five-deep on either side of the narrow walkway left for the players to pass through, surged forward to touch him in scenes normally reserved for international pop stars. Police officers and airport security staff had to form a circle around Beckham and escort him to the safety of the departure gate as hysterical supporters grabbed at his shirt.

Beckham returned from the Far East eighteen days later to pick up the keys to a top-of-the-range Audi, fruit of Real Madrid's sponsorship deal with the German car makers. The bulletproof

The top-of-the-range Audi, fruit of Real's sponsorship deal with the car manufacturers.

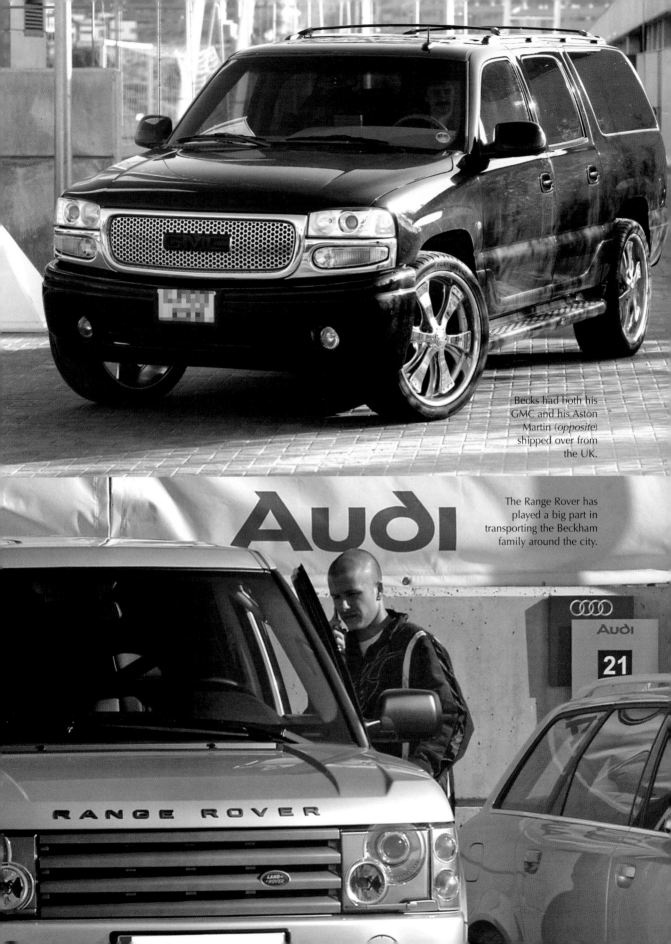

Becks had both his GMC and his Aston Martin (*opposite*) shipped over from the UK.

The Range Rover has played a big part in transporting the Beckham family around the city.

The crowning glory – Beckham pulls up in his Lamborghini, while onlookers cannot believe their eyes!

The England Captain grabbed the final goal at his first home game for
Real Madrid, versus Real Mallorca.

Brooklyn watches and celebrates as his dad scores for his new team.

vehicle – £61,000 to buy without extras – featured a state-of-the-art MMI computer, which enabled him to programme the car heating to start an hour before he wanted to use it during the cold Madrid winters. It also had an optional voice control system and infra-red sensor so the car would unlock automatically when David walked towards it with the keys in his pocket. And it didn't matter that wife Posh was very much her own woman – for the computer could be programmed so up to five people in the car could enjoy a different temperature and different seat position. It was to be one of half a dozen luxury cars Beckham drove during his first season at Madrid. He showed off his third left-hand drive just six weeks after signing for his new club when he roared out from his hotel car park in a £60,000 Porsche 911 Targa – a black two-door capable of 0–60mph in 6.3 seconds. Later in the year, he would have his Aston Martin and a gas-guzzling American import GMC shipped over from Britain.

Hard times at the Hard Rock – the couple leave the café through a back entrance in an effort to avoid the paparazzi.

When it came to bricks and mortar, things were not going so well. Beckham's search for somewhere to live began soon after he signed for Real Madrid, when he instructed estate agents to start looking for a property for him and his family. It was still going on in mid-October when he finally chanced upon the mansion that would become his base for the rest of the season.

In those three and a half months, Posh and Becks were shown around properties in most of Madrid's luxury suburbs. They included gems like the house called La Victoria near to their current home in the upmarket suburb of La Moraleja. Posh and Becks were also pictured walking up the steps of a £2.5-million mansion next to the king of Spain's home. Memorably, they viewed a £5-million mansion owned by the widow of a brutal South American dictator who had died of a heart attack while wanted for questioning over the murder of a political opponent. The palace boasted a nuclear bunker and a helicopter landing pad.

The couple's attempts to pinpoint somewhere to settle down became the subject of countless newspaper articles and comment pieces. It was said the

Brooklyn in the back of the Porsche which was crashed later that day by Posh and Becks look-alikes.

price was too high or Real Madrid had advised against the property for security reasons. Real Madrid security chiefs vetoed Victoria's 'yes' to a £3.6-million country mansion named El Bosque or 'The Wood' east of Madrid – for fear its isolated location would make David and his family kidnap targets. Increasingly, Victoria was blamed for being too fussy. She would veto a move on the grounds that the house in question was too small or not private enough. After a promising early start, some Real Madrid fans started to put the drop in Beckham's form on the pitch down to the fact he was still living out of a suitcase.

The lack of privacy that goes hand-in-hand with hotel life was demonstrated by the spate of run-ins between Beckham and the photographers who followed him day in, day out. The level of press interest in those first few weeks was always going to make it difficult for the England captain to go places and do things without someone behind him every step of the way.

The *Sun* and *Mirror* newspapers sent a full-time Beckham correspondent to Spain to bring readers the latest reports on David's life in the Spanish capital. They were each paired up with a photographer who also spent the rest of the year working almost exclusively on Beckham stories. That was without counting the freelance Spanish photographers who were prepared to work fourteen-hour days for a picture.

Being in a hotel made it ten times worse for David and his security advisers. There were only two exits, his private suite overlooked the road below, and even in an upmarket hotel like the Santo Mauro, people talk.

Beckham was accused of using his status when he and his Spanish-speaking former assistant, Andy Bernal, stopped in front of a police station a couple of streets away from the hotel and called on armed cops to stop two chasing cars from tailing them. What Bernal said remains a mystery – but the incident ended with Beckham driving off in his Porsche, two Spanish paparazzi being charged with insulting the police and ordered to appear in court and one of the photographers claiming police had told them afterwards that the England captain thought they were terrorists.

During another pursuit, Beckham was let into Moncloa Palace – the equivalent of London's Buckingham Palace – so he could escape the press. The police were

Arriving at Malaga with the team, ahead of their game with Malaga FC.

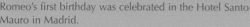
Romeo's first birthday was celebrated in the Hotel Santo Mauro in Madrid.

also called in to deal with claims that one of Beckham's minders had indecently assaulted a female reporter during a scuffle – and an allegation that David had deliberately driven at a photographer outside his hotel as he tried to take his photograph. However, nothing came of this claim.

But the most bizarre moment involving the Beckham camp and the press came on 31 August 2003 when David and Victoria look-alikes tried to give Spanish paparazzi the slip – and ended up crashing the Real Madrid star's Porsche. It followed a first birthday party earlier that day for Romeo, which led to

police being called amid accusations David had thrown water over a photographer. The stunt was designed to ensure the real Posh and Becks could slip out afterwards in a second car and enjoy a quiet night out. But it backfired spectacularly after the sports car smashed into a beaten-up Ford Escort as it sped out of the Santo Mauro's underground hotel car park. Driver Andy Bernal – at the wheel of David's car in a white tank top with a baseball cap pulled tightly over his eyes Beckham-style – reversed back into the car park almost as quickly as he had emerged. Strangely, the Spaniard whose Ford Escort was damaged in the crash

went into the hotel lobby shouting he was going to make David and Victoria pay – then emerged twenty minutes later refusing to speak.

While Beckham's relationship with certain sections of the press was not good, he certainly had Real Madrid's fans on his side. Two goals from his first two home games and a string of breathtaking passes won him the hearts of his new side's supporters. And he won the admiration of Madrid's five and a half million population with his constant praise of the city and its relaxed lifestyle. To their delight, son Brooklyn was invariably pictured wearing a pint-sized version of his dad's Real Madrid shirt.

Beckham's decision to celebrate son Romeo's first birthday in the Spanish capital – albeit with a garden party for twenty family and friends in the grounds of the Santo Mauro – also enamoured him to his growing army of fans. Even when he failed to maintain promising early performances and suffered an alarming dip in form before the year was out, patient Real Madrid fans called for him to be given more time to settle in.

But if David scored ten out of ten in the popularity stakes, Victoria was struggling to make any mark at all. In a country where family is sacred, the

Left: Victoria was accused of not spending enough time in Madrid – and the time she did spend in the city was often spent in the designer shops.

former Spice Girl raised eyebrows by her refusal to move to Spain full-time and by the handful of days she spent in the country each month. When she was around, she only seemed to be interested in using her plastic in Madrid's chic designer shops. Famously, she was also said to have claimed she didn't like Madrid because the city lacked glamour and smelled of garlic and cocido – a local dish of boiled meat and vegetables. Victoria has always denied the comments – attributed to a friend and widely reported in the Spanish press – but it damaged her reputation.

In an article appearing in national newspaper *La Razon* soon after Beckham signed for Real Madrid, Cecilia Garcia wrote, 'I can imagine her shopping in Madrid, walking with her head down and thinking, "What am I doing here with this bunch of euros that look like Monopoly money when I could be in Oxford Street?" Posh Spice has become "Stray Spice", in search of an oasis where she can exhaust her hunger for consumerism, distinction and glamour.' The same newspaper labelled her 'surly' and 'unsociable' after her first public appearance at the *Elle* magazine style awards in September. Opinion writer Jorge Berlanga claimed Victoria must have been 'smelling manure' by the look on her face. David, it seemed, could do nothing wrong … Victoria nothing right.

Victoria picks up her *Elle* award for Fashionable Woman of the Year. One Spanish newspaper claimed she was 'surly' and 'unsociable' after she attended this event.

Becks with his Spanish homework.

36

Brotherly love. Brooklyn and Romeo adjust to life in the new city with a trip to a Madrid theme park.

Home Sweet Home

After what seemed like an eternal four months played out in magazines and newspapers, David and Victoria finally found what they were looking for and moved into their first proper Madrid home at the start of November 2003. If security and a bit of peace and quiet were what they wanted, they had picked well. The £4.5-million mansion was on an upmarket private estate known as Las Encinas – 'The Oaks' in English – some fifteen miles northwest of the city centre. Another two miles of road running through woodland surrounding the estate separated the Beckhams' pad from the main entrance.

The entrance – protected by heavy wrought-iron electronic gates and a second security barrier – was manned night and day. Security guards patrolled the estate and spy cameras provided further back-up. And several dirt tracks leading on to the back of the estate offered David an easy escape route when he wanted to leave unseen and avoid paparazzi waiting for him on the main road outside. As if that wasn't enough, the Beckhams also called in a private firm to upgrade security around their new home. The result was more CCTV and a pair of Rottweilers who slept in kennels in the garden – in short, a fortress that enabled David to enjoy the haven that had eluded him during his enforced hotel stay.

The house itself was equally impressive – heated outdoor pool, floodlit tennis court, 2.7 acres of private

Home Sweet Home – the new villa in which the family put down their Spanish roots.

Moving in.

woodland and five bedrooms with en-suite bathrooms. Not that it was up for rent or sale when Posh and Becks fell in love with it while viewing a house belonging to a Spanish marquis on the same small enclave of just over half a dozen mansions. In the world of what David wants, David gets, he is said to have approached the owner and made her an offer she couldn't refuse. The offer was £32,000 a month.

The owner – a French publicist and his Spanish TV presenter wife Ana Garcia-Sineriz – agreed straight away and downsized to a nearby flat with their two children so the Beckhams could move in. David admitted he was relieved to have found somewhere to live – even if it was on a six-month contract ending the following May. At a press conference soon after the move he confessed, 'Finding a house is always important. I've spent three months in a hotel and the staff there treated me wonderfully. Being in a hotel hasn't stopped me concentrating on my football. But you always feel better and more settled when you're in your own home with your own family.'

Except Beckham was often alone in his own home – sometimes thousands of miles away from Victoria and the children. The number of days the former Spice Girl spent in the Spanish capital each month could be counted on the fingers of one hand. Brooklyn had been

expected to enrol at a private English-language school in Madrid at the end of summer 2003. Instead, he continued to attend lessons at his old school in Hertfordshire and commuted between Spain and the UK by private jet to see his dad from time to time.

While Beckham was in a hotel, Victoria's absence was more under-standable. But with her husband now installed at Las Encinas, the amount of time Posh spent in England was raising more and more eyebrows. The first hints of trouble had already appeared with paparazzi pictures of David and his now-famous PA Rebecca Loos gazing into each other's eyes during a night out at Madrid nightspot Ananda while Victoria was out of town.

Rumours of problems grew with reports the couple had rowed over Victoria's friendship with rap producer Damon Dash. Beckham responded by issuing a statement saying he and his wife were 'extremely happy together as a family'. And he denied speculation Victoria was unhappy in Madrid at a press conference where he spoke of his relief at finding a new home.

'In spite of what people say, my wife is very happy and likes Spain a lot,' he told reporters. 'The thing is that because of her work she has to spend a lot of time away in London and America.'

Whatever the truth of his comments, the timing couldn't have been worse.

Happy with her new home, Victoria is all smiles as she leaves a Madrid restaurant.

School's out for Brooklyn. When the family looked around exclusive schools in Madrid, it was expected that he would begin classes – he didn't enrol until the following year.

The very day they appeared in British newspapers, Romeo hit and cut his head in a fall at the new home. David gave him first aid before rushing him to hospital for stitches to the wound. Victoria was 3,000 miles away in New York and was told the news on the phone. And just over a week later the *Sunday Mirror* went 'world exclusive' with the claim that Victoria had told David during a row the marriage was over unless he returned to Britain.

In a memorable turn of phrase she is said to have delivered the ultimatum with the words, 'It's my way or the highway.' The couple went to the Press Complaints Commission over the piece. The organisation – the newspaper industry's self-regulating body – failed to come to a decision over the complaint.

Beckham's choice of friends to help him while away the hours when Victoria was out of town hardly helped when it came to discounting rumours that his marriage was heading for the rocks. Roberto Carlos – a man with a fondness for Madrid's nightlife, on the rebound following his marriage split from Alexandra Pinheiro – became David's best friend that first season. The pair were often pictured out together. One of their favourite haunts was the Asador Donostiarra, a popular Basque restaurant where several photos signed by David, his teammates and national and international celebrities hang on the wall. Another Real Madrid player Beckham became close to was Ronaldo, also a lover of the good life, whose split from wife Milene Dominguez soon after David joined Real Madrid produced headlines but little surprise.

It was at Ronaldo's infamous twenty-seventh birthday party in September 2003 that Beckham met Spanish supermodel Esther Canadas – of whom more later… Paparazzi photographers took hundreds of pictures of model-like women walking through the gates of Ronaldo's mansion – but none of Victoria who was in London and whose only contact with David that night was by telephone.

And Becks got his first ticking off over his bachelor-boy lifestyle after a night out with Ronaldo at trendy nightclub Shabay, ahead of a crucial derby match. The pair headed for the club after returning to Madrid from a disappointing away draw against Osasuna at the end of November 2003 in which Beckham limped off early through injury. They didn't arrive at the fashionable nightspot until 4.15am. No sign, once again, of Victoria, who was thought to be in London.

The late-night sortie ended up with Beckham being named and shamed in a regular section in daily newspaper *La Razon* devoted to the day's heroes and villains. Laying into the England captain in its editorial, the paper sentenced, 'No one can deny Beckham's phenomenal achievements since his arrival at Real Madrid. But his performances can't justify other excesses or mistakes. That's why Madrid's supporters don't understand what the Englishman was doing at Madrid nightclub Shabay at 4.30am on Sunday morning, after coming off early against Osasuna with an injury and when he was set to face

David looked to teammates such as Roberto Carlos for companionship, as Victoria was not a permanent fixture in Spain.

A Real Madrid night on the town. Figo with Helen Swedin (*right*), Zidane (*below right*) and Ronaldo (*this page*) enjoying a meal at favourite Spanish haunt Asador Donostiarra.

Teammates Roberto Carlos (above) and Ronaldo (below) helped
David settle in to a new team and a new city.

Becks with teammates at the launch of the Pepsi ad in which the Real team starred.

Atletico de Madrid in a derby match on Wednesday. A disco doesn't seem the best place to recover.'

Beckham spoke glowingly about his two friends in a radio interview he gave just before Christmas 2003 – shortly after a flying trip back to Britain to receive his OBE from the Queen.

'Ronnie speaks a bit of English and we communicate very well on the football field. He's a fantastic person,' he said.

'And Roberto has treated me like his son or brother since I arrived.'

Asked about life as one of the world's most photographed couples, Becks said,

'Generally we live well and we can't complain. We feel it's better to enjoy the situation and everything that comes with it. You either accept you're famous or you suffer. We both feel very lucky, we have an incredible family and, although we come up against things we don't like, they all form part of the package that being David and Victoria involves.'

Admitting he had become a night bird, he added, 'In Spain people have lunch and dinner a lot later. But I've got used to the timetable now. When I return to England I will have to eat alone at midnight.'

The *galactico* helps to spread Christmas cheer in Madrid by visiting children in hospital with Raul, Guti and basketball player Alberto Herreros.

Minder

Cuban heavy Delfin Fernandez and his friends looked like they'd stepped off the set of *Reservoir Dogs* the day they walked into David Beckham's life. Shades, dark suits over white shirts, BMWs with blacked-out windows and CVs fitting of Quentin Tarantino's film rogues. Four English bodyguards with thick Mancunian accents provided close personal security for David, Victoria and their boys during the first weeks of his move to Spain. They spoke very little, smiled even less and largely remained a mystery for the photographers who followed them and Beckham round.

Delfin was a different ball game – and hours into his arrival was laying down his credentials for the job to anyone within earshot. Old Trafford

seemed a long way away as he recounted outside David's Madrid hotel how he spent fifteen years working as a spy for Communist dictator Fidel Castro under the codename Otto. With a hi-tech array of hidden microphones and video cameras six-footer Fernandez would record every word and movement of high-profile visitors to Cuba for the nation's counter-intelligence Department 11, so the regime could blackmail them if required. Delfin delighted in recalling how he was so close to Fidel that the dictator entrusted him with the task of finding him his pet Rottweiler because of his contacts abroad.

When a man with his career history tells you, 'Where I come from, people disappear if they get in the way,' as Delfin often did, it makes you want to be nice to him.

The Cubans were hired to strengthen security following a string of bust-ups between Beckham's English-speaking entourage and the mainly Spanish-speaking paparazzi pack. Becks must have hoped the fact they spoke the language would help to ease the tensions that had developed between the two sides. The relationship lasted less than six months. It was short, far from sweet and backfired spectacularly as Delfin went public on the months at his beck-and-call to allege the England captain enjoyed a series of extra-marital flings, all hotly denied and none ever substantiated.

The Cubans arrived on the scene in autumn 2003 while David was still at the Santo Mauro. The hotel, already heaving from the daily attention of fans and photographers, started to look like a president's palace as the doormen and David's shaven-headed English body-guards were joined by the suited and booted hardmen from La Havana.

When he wasn't at the entrance to the Santo Mauro, walkie-talkie in his hand,

Delfin Fernandez (top left) and Arsenio (top right) were two of the Cuban minders drafted in to protect the Beckhams. Fernandez was often seen at the wheel of the family cars.

Delfin quickly became a familiar sight at the wheel of Becks's Range Rover as he shadowed him night and day in the city. He made sure he wasn't followed from training, he accompanied him to ad shoots and he'd be by David's side when he went out to eat. Delfin was at the five-star Ritz Hotel overseeing security the night Becks spent £1,200 on a three-course meal and wine for Victoria in a private room he had decked out with candles and flowers. And two days later he was helping them slip out of a back door after a late lunch at Madrid's Hard Rock Café, where the couple saved their pennies with a cheeseburger and onion rings washed down with diet Pepsi.

David even entrusted Delfin with the task of compiling a report on security at Runnymede College, the English-language school the Beckhams ended up sending son Brooklyn to. It seemed like Fidel's ex-secret service agent and his team had won the confidence of their new multi-millionaire paymasters, especially when they continued to guard David after his move to his new home. The reality was somewhat different.

Tension between Becks's two sets of bodyguards had been mounting for

Security around
Victoria and the
children was always
extremely high.

Delfin shadowing the couple as they try to avoid the press at the Hard Rock Café in Madrid.

some time. The English regarded the Cubans as big-mouthed show-offs who spent too much time joking around with the press pack. The Cubans saw the English as a bunch of amateur 'yes men' who, for the most part, didn't have a clue about how to protect their clients.

David might have been happy enough with the Cuban connection. The problem for Fidel's former men was they weren't very popular with Victoria and her family. Posh blamed the Cubans for helping to lead David astray in Madrid and decided she wanted someone she could rely on to keep an eye on him during her long absences from the Spanish capital. Victoria and powerful dad Tony eventually ordered him and his team out.

The Beckhams were mistaken if they thought that, by firing Delfin, they were getting rid of a problem. The unusually high profile he acquired working as David's bodyguard was nothing compared to the name he was about to make for himself as a free agent. The Beckhams had Delfin and his team sign confidentiality agreements, which should, in theory, have prevented them from speaking while they were still alive. But, inexplicably, the signatures on the agreements postdated the start of their employment by several weeks. And Delfin argued that the agreements were invalid because the Beckhams owed them unpaid wages when they

fired them. Delfin also talks of a mystery tape in his safekeeping that is his 'life insurance'. True or not, the validity of the agreements have never been tested. David and Victoria have consistently failed to try to silence Delfin through the courts.

The Cuban was the obvious call for journalists after he and the Beckhams parted ways – and again when Rebecca Loos unleashed the showbiz story of the year in April 2004 by claiming she had enjoyed an affair with David, a claim always dismissed as ridiculous by the Beckhams. In the weeks before the story broke, Delfin met journalists from at least two British tabloids and discussed deals with several others through an assistant.

I was present at a meeting in Madrid between Delfin and a *Sunday People* reporter at the end of January 2004. Beckham's former man stripped us of recording equipment before demanding £600,000 to put the paper in touch with a series of girls he claimed the England captain had slept with – claims never accepted by David and, in any event, the two failed to reach a deal – although the paper went on to publish details of the meeting in a back room at Madrid's Planet Hollywood restaurant under the headline 'Beck-trayal'.

Delfin met up with representatives from The *Sun* in Malaga when the Rebecca Loos story broke. The minder, now working for Hollywood actor Antonio Banderas, revealed David and Rebecca shared their first kiss on the back seat of the car he was driving as he chauffeured Beckham back to his hotel. But he chose Spanish TV to officially 'break cover' in June 2004 and spoke openly for the first time about what he alleged was going on behind closed doors while he worked for David. He backed Rebecca Loos's claim of an affair, insisted reports David had cheated on Victoria with a Spanish supermodel were true and went on to tell how Becks had bedded a string of brunettes he cherrypicked on nights out in Madrid. These claims have been rubbished by the Beckhams.

Asked why he had decided to speak out, Delfin claimed it was because Beckham still owed him money. He told late night programme *Donde Estas Corazon* on Spain's Antena 3, 'There was one point when we were owed three months. We had to pay for everything up front out of our own pocket, telephone, parking, meals and then claim it back. The situation was getting intolerable. I spoke to David while we were waiting for Victoria to fly in last December and said we were considering going to court. His attitude was, "Go ahead and sue me. I am God." I'm still owed money. I'm not going to quote figures but it's an important amount.'

David takes some time out from training to play ball with his sons – the pictures of him sporting a dummy attracted much media attention.

Brooklyn demonstrates he shares his mum's sense of style.

Becks, Sex and Texts

It might not be in the same league as the day JFK died or John Lennon got shot. But for Posh and Becks 4 April 2004 is a day they're not likely to forget in a hurry. Sundays are usually slow news days and editors will tell you that filling the pages of Monday's newspaper can often be a bit of a struggle. Rebecca Loos made sure she turned the first Sunday of that April into one of the busiest news days of the year by sensationally claiming David cheated on Victoria with her.

Grainy video images showing her cosying up to David on an evening out in a Madrid bar had already been published in the *News of the World* at the end of September 2003. Rebecca was named in the report as the woman Becks was most probably with that

night. The man who took the video might well have been an ardent Beckham fan as the *News of the World* chose to describe him. But he was first and foremost a Spanish paparazzi whose video footage ended up being flown across to London and sold for thousands of pounds.

The public silence of the Beckhams' aide at the time – and the fact the paper could only insinuate naughtiness with a classic 'What will Posh say?' headline – left David facing few questions after he put out a joint statement with his wife insisting everything was fine. Posh and Becks were all smiles that afternoon when they went out for a spin in David's £80,000 soft-top Aston Martin – shipped out from England to add to his collection of luxury cars. And that night a marriage crisis seemed the last thing on their minds as Becks treated his wife to a romantic dinner at Madrid's five-star Ritz Hotel.

There was no insinuation on pages one to seven of the *News of the World*'s edition that 4 April. It didn't need to imply anything. Rebecca Loos – now the Beckhams' former aide after David's parting of ways with sports management company SFX – had given an interview to the paper claiming they had had a secret torrid affair.

David's public image was that of the perfect family man. Advertisers who had paid out millions of pounds to secure his services had played on his looks and undoubted status as a sex symbol. But their love affair with Beckham came equally, if not more, from his standing as the faithful father-of-two who loved his wife and, when he wasn't turning in man-of-the-match performances on the pitch, was keeping out of trouble off the pitch. The advertising clout they were looking for didn't come from a roll between the sheets with a self-confessed bisexual in the hotel bed where he slept with his wife when she was in town. Nor did it come from the series of lurid text messages he was said to have sent Rebecca, printed over a full page in the *News of the World*.

The paper therefore hit the nail on the head when it billed its exclusive as 'the story you thought you'd never read'. It was the talk of dinner tables up and down the country and dominated every news agenda of the day. The previous night, seven members of a terrorist gang linked to the Madrid train bombings had blown themselves up after killing a policeman during a siege. I boarded a plane to Madrid early Sunday morning to cover the aftermath. But one hour later, after landing, I was listening to the first of nine messages from news desks asking me to work on the Beckham story. Daily newspapers sent over their own staff reporters and photographers during the course of the morning. It was a turning point for David Beckham and his family as they entered the ninth month of his Spanish adventure. For Rebecca Loos – who made £350,000 from the interview but lost the anonymity she had enjoyed for the first twenty-six years of her life – things were never going to be the same again either.

Victoria, who had received some of the blame for not spending enough time with Becks in Madrid, jetted to the Alps from London for a skiing holiday with her family on the day the story appeared. David, on club duty with Real Madrid and thousands of miles away from his wife, flew out to join her the following day. Rebecca Loos remained holed up with a *News of the World* reporter at a secret location so the paper

Following the publication of the image of Rebecca Loos and Beckham in a nightclub together, Victoria and David went out for a spin in his Aston Martin to show the world that all was well.

When the Beckhams first arrived in Spain, Rebecca Loos was often in evidence in photographs of them in and around the city.

could keep her away from its tabloid rivals and prepare for 'Beckhamgate' week two. With the protagonists deserting Madrid as British reporters arrived in the city to look for stories to write, Rebecca's brother found himself holding the front line.

John Loos was still asleep when the first of the reporters buzzed on the intercom at the family home in an upmarket suburb to the north of the city centre. You'd expect a sister to warn her brother she was about to claim an icon like David Beckham had cheated on his wife with her. But John was like a rabbit caught in the headlights as it became apparent the press were telling him something he couldn't quite get his head around. Only after he made a quick call to Rebecca on her mobile and she confirmed her story to him did the penny seem to drop.

So unprepared was her family for what was to come, they hadn't even taken the mobile numbers down from the back window of Rebecca's for-sale

car parked outside her home. One belonged to the Beckhams' former aide, the other to her brother. That day their phones rang all day with reporters trying to pretend they were interested in buying a Mini before coming clean and trying to get fresh quotes on the allegations threatening to derail the Posh and Becks marriage.

The Rebecca Loos incident opened the floodgates to allegations that Beckham had had affairs. Esther Canadas's name had first been linked to David the previous autumn after local media covering Real Madrid striker Ronaldo's twenty-seventh birthday party claimed they had disappeared into an upstairs bedroom together during the bash. Now the Spanish supermodel became front-page news again as Rebecca also claimed Esther had been his lover. Both claims were flatly denied by Beckham. Pressmen went to the Madrid school where Canadas drops her adopted child off in the mornings to try to speak to her. They waited outside her home in the hope of encouraging her to break her silence. More than one reporter was dispatched to her home town of Alicante on Spain's east coast to track down her father and find out what he had to say.

During that mad month when arguably more newspaper columns were dedicated to David Beckham than at any time when he was living in England, one UK Sunday newspaper offered Esther Canadas a staggering £100,000 for an exclusive interview. Her agent rejected the offer outright. Esther wasn't going to talk about her private life, she said. Up until today she has never spoken.

Other women were less backward in coming forward. Enter Australian model Sarah Marbeck, twenty-nine, who told the *News of the World* she had had a two-year affair with Beckham that started during a Manchester United tour to Singapore in July 2001. Beckham totally refuted this allegation, as well as calling it ludicrous. She was later exposed as a former prostitute who once worked for a high-class escort agency in Sydney. Enter Celina Laurie, twenty-seven, who told the *People* newspaper that she had sex with Beckham in August 2002 in the Danish

The Mini that Rebecca Loos was trying to sell. Her family were unaware of what was about to come out in the press and the 'for sale' sign displaying both her and her brother's mobile numbers was still in evidence as the story broke.

EN PORTADA

Sarah Marbeck, la aventura malaya de Beckham

interviú

A displeased-looking Victoria watches as an advertisement for an interview with Sarah Marbeck – who claimed to have had an affair with Beckham – was displayed at the Real Madrid v Barcelona match.

city of Aarhus after a Manchester United game there. Beckham has never commented publicly on this allegation. Re-enter the fray Spanish party girl Nuria Bermudez. She famously claimed to have slept with half the Real Madrid squad soon after David signed for the club. Now she seized the chance to repeat earlier claims the British press had largely ignored that Becks had already bedded her.

Nuria, twenty-six, even went one further and claimed – without offering any evidence – that since he moved to Madrid Beckham's conquests, apart from her and Victoria, were virtually into the double figures. Beckham refused to give these allegations any credence by commenting on them. It was an astonishing assertion – and one that still hadn't settled when a mystery redhead called Helia went on Spanish TV to say Becks had romped with an unnamed blonde friend in a toilet at the Buddha Bar in Madrid, where a year later the England captain would celebrate his thirtieth birthday.

A few weeks later Delfin Fernandez

Loos giving an interview on Spanish television.

would go into intimate detail on Spanish TV about the role he alleges he played in his former client's love life. Delfin named three 'normal Spanish girls' he claimed David had bedded during nights out in Madrid. Detailing how he helped undress them and checked them for recording equipment before sending them into the star's bedroom, he said, 'None of the women who went with him were coerced in any way. They were told exactly what searches they had to go through before they could see David. I'd get them to hand in shoes, belts, we'd take the shoulder straps off their dresses, anything that could be used to hurt David. And we'd take off them all their accessories. I'd take the batteries off their mobiles and anything that could be used as recording equipment.

'Basically David would be on a night out, he'd pick a girl he liked the look of and send me over to talk to them. No one ever said no. Everyone went home happy.'

Beckham never commented publicly on Delfin's allegations.

The flurry of claims about David's off-the-pitch activities split the press and public into two camps. Rebecca Loos became the 'sleazy senorita' to some. To others she was the victim of a failed marriage whose former employer had slept with her and then sacked her. The Beckhams have never sued over Rebecca's repeated insistence she had

an affair with David – although the claims have been denied by him. Text messages provided by Loos to the *News of the World* as evidence of a fling to support her claims were also disputed by Beckham.

Barcelona-based singer Rebecca Pous, long bereft of chart success after a hit that stayed at number one in the Spanish charts for five weeks, was claimed by a third person to have had an 'encounter' with Beckham in a hotel. Confronted by a Spanish TV crew, she refused to answer their questions. The footballer never commented on this claim.

Things started getting really out of hand for the Beckhams when a Spanish national newspaper claimed Victoria's family had hired an Israeli private detective to look into claims David romped with Rebecca Loos and Esther Canadas. He reportedly spent six days in Madrid quizzing security staff, hotel chefs, drivers, security workers, cooks and other people close to Beckham. The newspaper, *El Mundo*, described the private eye's paymaster as a fifty-year-old female relative of Victoria's.

The story, largely ignored by the British press who simply didn't believe it, left David's fans with the impression it was open season on the England captain and anything would go. The Beckhams knew they had to do something to counter the bad press they were getting. The fight back was about to kick in...

Fighting Back

In a world where presentation and spin play a key role in real wars, media wars are no different. Victoria Beckham might not be the world's greatest singer – but even her severest critics recognise her ability to turn a negative into a positive, or at least a non-negative.

David branded the Rebecca Loos allegations 'ludicrous' in a statement issued the day after they appeared. He insisted, 'I am very happily married, have a wonderful wife and two very special kids. There is nothing that any third party can do to change these facts.'

But what had more impact than any of David's words were the pictures of him and Victoria together over the following fortnight – first in the French Alps and then in Spain. Two days after

Rebecca's claims first appeared, a radiant Becks was photographed giving his wife a piggy-back in the snow outside their £20,000-a-week chalet in the French ski resort of Courchevel. The show of affection, described as 'staged' even by the Beckham-friendly *Sun*, was more in tune with a honeymoon than a marriage crisis brought on by the cheating of a husband and the refusal of his wife to up sticks and live with him in a foreign country.

The smiles continued when the couple returned to Spain. First they were seen as a happy family by taking sons Brooklyn and Romeo for a pizza lunch before stopping to sign autographs as they bought fruit from a Madrid greengrocers' (also frequented by

As the Rebecca Loos scandal broke across the world, these pictures of the family enjoying themselves were taken in Madrid.

Spain's royal family). Later that day they took the children to a park near their Madrid home. At one point David and Victoria shared a tender embrace at the bottom of the slide as the children played under the watchful eye of the England captain's minders. For almost the first time since they were in Madrid, photographers Rolando Cardenoso and Ramon Perez Sanroman, who had followed Posh and Becks since they arrived in Spain, were given virtual free reign to take the snaps they wanted.

Even the couple's pet dog – a £600 Sharpei pup named Carlos after former Real Madrid manager Carlos Queiroz – appeared in the pictures. And the following day, to the delight of waiting photographers, David and Victoria walked arm in arm into a petrol station opposite their home before the England captain left for a training break with his Real Madrid teammates in La Manga. Posh took lots of stick over what appeared to be an orchestrated PR campaign to get pictures of her and her husband together in the papers – and keep Rebecca Loos and the other women out. The *Daily Mirror* – under the uncompromising headline 'The Becks Sex Scandal: Day 11' – ran a series of photos of Victoria grinning like a Cheshire cat on what should have been some of the worst days of her life. Pictures showing a publicly united David and Victoria made the papers every day for nearly two weeks.

Rebecca Loos hit back with a Sky TV interview that took her earnings off the back of her Beckham claims to around half a million pounds. But by then the 'Sleazy Senorita' label invented by the

Sun was beginning to grow on a public who saw Posh and Becks as getting a rough deal. Rebecca would become the victim of anonymous death threats. Her family ended up having to install CCTV cameras at their Madrid home after waking up one morning to find a dead rabbit outside their front door.

For his hardcore fans, David could never do anything wrong. But the Beckhams' attempts to fight back with their own publicity machine went a long way towards winning over the waverers...

Around the same time, David shaved

Victoria and David present a united front at a party shortly after the Rebecca Loos scandal broke. Beckham is sporting his newly shaved head.

his shoulder-length hair off in the latest in a long line of image changes that have seen the England captain feted as a king of fashion. Becks showed off his new skinhead at a party in London in mid-April before flying back to Spain to rejoin his Real Madrid teammates. The England captain called in his hairdresser the same day the *News of the World* claimed David and Victoria were considering a trial separation. This was in the third of the paper's three weeks of front pages on the Beckhams, which started with the Rebecca Loos exclusive.

The couple showed admirable togetherness by dismissing the story as 'rubbish'. The real reason David cut his hair was for a photo shoot for Police sunglasses later that week. The advert was not due out until the following year but it meant Becks had to decide on the style he wanted so he could easily match it when the new campaign was released. But it had the effect of propelling them back into the papers as David arrived for the party sporting his new look – just an hour after Rebecca Loos grabbed her own headlines with another TV

A shopping trip in Madrid. Victoria holds up a lock of David's hair to the press and photographers.

appearance on the *Richard & Judy* show.

Marks & Spencer announced it was ditching Beckham that summer. The £10-million contract for his DB07 boys' wear range was not extended when it came up for renewal. The move was jumped on as a sign David's brand value had been damaged by the allegations of infidelity. His poor form on the football pitch – and mediocre performances at Euro 2004 – didn't help. But his contract with Vodafone was renewed. His appearance as a gladiator in an epic Pepsi advert was rated as the ad that had most mentions in newspapers all year. And in May 2004 Beckham agreed a multi-million-pound three-year advertising deal to become the face of shaving giant Gillette.

Research carried out in the UK at the time suggested the string of allegations relating to extra-marital affairs had had some negative impact, but probably not enough to make Beckham a sponsorship liability. The pulling power the England captain still retained was perhaps best demonstrated by the amount of money a

Opposite: Little Brooklyn waves to the pitch from the stand. He proudly sports the same number as his dad's international shirt.

Attending the funeral of the mother of Real Madrid President Florentino Perez.

A new tattoo – Becks's neck sports a crucifix with wings.

The £2000-a-night Amenjena resort in Marrakech.

Spanish soft drinks salesman made from the Becks Euro 2004 penalty ball. Beckham blasted the ball into the stands during a quarter-final penalty shoot-out against Portugal, which the host nation went on to win 6–5. The ball was caught by Coca-Cola salesman Pablo Carral, who had travelled from his home in northwest Spain to watch the match.

I travelled to Galicia at the end of June to try and buy the ball for a UK newspaper that ended up offering Carral, aged twenty-five, more than £10,000 plus a share of the profits from an auction of the ball. Pablo, knowing he was on to a good thing, hired a solicitor to help him negotiate the best deal and put the football in a safe before meeting me for dinner to discuss the proposal. It is a sure sign that someone's popularity rating is not at a low ebb when a paper is ready to part with a five-figure sum for a round piece of leather whose only claim to fame is that it has had his boot on it.

Try telling Pablo Carral that David Beckham was a broken man, a social pariah whose status as an icon had been irreparably damaged by the allegations he had cheated on his wife. He turned down the equivalent of nearly a year's wages and the promise of more from a newspaper-organised auction to put the ball up for sale on Internet auction site eBay. The football ended up going for nearly £19,000 to a Canadian online casino that subsequently took the ball on a world tour, including a trip into space. Pablo was presented with his cheque at the Santo Mauro Hotel, which was at the centre of so many of the sex claims made against Beckham…

Pablo was still receiving bids when Posh and Becks were photographed during a romantic break in Marrakech. The *Sunday Mirror* claimed at the time the couple were in the Moroccan city to renew their marriage vows to coincide with their fifth wedding anniversary. The couple picked a £2,000-a-night apartment – with its own swimming pool and walled courtyard with lemon trees and a fountain – at the Amenjena resort twelve miles from the city centre. They also had a personal butler on call and the use of two first-class restaurants, a gym and a health spa. The couple reportedly called off their plans to renew their vows at the last minute and disappeared from their luxury hotel resort as half a dozen British journalists headed for Marrakech.

They would later surface at Elton John's home in the south of France – before heading back to the same exclusive resort in Morocco another six weeks later for a second seventy-two-hour visit. Whatever the truth behind their trip to Africa, the facts were incontrovertible as David's first season with Real Madrid came to a close. The Beckhams might have had every inch of their relationship put under the microscope during a testing year that had seen both David's fidelity and Victoria's commitment to Spain and her husband called into question. But they were still together – for better or for worse. And whatever the nature of their relationship behind closed doors, in public David and Victoria didn't look like a couple on the verge of a breakdown.

David Beckham dons local headdress in an attempt to mingle whilst shopping for bargains with Victoria and a translator in Marrakech's famous souk.

Dad takes some time out from training to have a kickaround with his boys.

Spectating with ex-EastEnder and author Tom Watt.

United they stand …

A New Chapter

David Beckham bowed out of Euro 2004 a dejected figure with two missed penalties and a string of disappointing performances to cap a testing few months off the pitch. His football was being questioned and his leadership skills were being placed under the microscope. It wasn't only the suntan he picked up in Morocco and the Cote d'Azur that made him look like a different man when he took to the pitch for the start of Real Madrid pre-season training in mid-July.

Beckham blamed his poor Euro 2004 performances on the previous training regime under ex-Real Madrid manager Carlos Queiroz. But successor Jose Antonio Camacho, Spain's former national coach, looked like he would give Beckham no cause for concern. He worked the club's stars into the ground at the training camp in the Andalucian city of Jerez. Michael Schumacher was among the Formula One stars practising at the race track next door as Beckham and his pals trained. But Camacho made sure his highly paid stars focused on their football and they didn't step near the track to take time out and watch the German burn rubber. And David quickly dispelled any doubts over his fitness levels by coming through the gruelling eighty-minute morning training session in 26°C heat with flying colours.

Becks was the biggest draw for the hundreds of fans who had to apply at the town hall for tickets to watch the training sessions. And the relaxed England

Off to pre-season training in Jerez.

Regaining form before the new season.

captain would often stop the golf buggy ferrying him between the training pitch and his five-star accommodation at the Montecastillo Hotel, in the shadow of the Jerez race track, so he could sign autographs. He even took it in the spirit of things when the visiting city mayor, Maria Jose Garcia Pelayo, perhaps overcome by the odour from Beckham's sun lotion, told him he smelled of coconut in an undiplomatic outburst that left his teammates in stitches.

The beginning of the new season would certainly bring the winds of change with it. For a start there was a new home to look forward to. The Beckhams had left their old place in May and put their stuff in storage, ready for the move at the start of David's second season in Spain. The location of their new pad was revealed in early September after the England captain returned from his club's pre-season tour of the Far East. They picked a new area – the posh Madrid suburb of

La Moraleja, ten miles northeast of the city centre and some twenty-five minutes' drive from El Plantio, where they had rented their first home. The neighbourhood was already home to Brazilian teammate Ronaldo and dozens of Spanish celebrities, including bullfighters and actors. Michael Owen and fiancée-now-wife Louise Bonsall would also end up there when they moved to Madrid.

Football idol. It was Beckham who drew the fans at the pre-season training session. He found time to speak to fans and sign autographs.

Living there you could enjoy the privacy of a large home with two to three acres of land that typified the walled and gated properties lining the quiet, residential streets of the sprawling neighbourhood. At the same time the centre of the city was a little less than half an hour's drive from La Moraleja, making it close enough for residents in this most exclusive of Madrid addresses to enjoy the benefits of a capital city and escape the downsides.

The house the Beckhams settled on was just down the road from the mansion

In action for Real against Krakow.

owned by the widow of a south American dictator that they had viewed the previous year. Ironically, it was next door to the mansion called La Victoria that Posh had also given the once-over during the couple's mammoth search for a home when they first arrived in Madrid.

The Beckhams' new place had four floors and boasted five bedrooms with en-suite bathrooms, a games room, a large outdoor swimming pool and a tennis court. A garage with space for six cars occupied most of the ground floor. A lift connected the garages to the first two floors. Floor one had a large dining room and living room, kitchen, servants' living quarters and two bathrooms. The five bedrooms were all on the second floor, with the games room occupying most of the third-floor loft conversion. The red-brick house, set in a quiet tree-lined avenue, was surrounded by manicured lawns and nearly two acres of woodland. A long porch with tables and chairs, where Posh and Becks could eat out on warm evenings, ran alongside the rectangular swimming pool behind the house. Pine and oak trees and a six-foot wall running round the perimeter screened the property from the road.

In the days before the Beckhams moved in, security staff put in extra CCTV cameras and raised the perimeter fence to make sure all but the house

The couple bought this stunning villa in the upmarket development 'La Moraleja' in the suburbs of Madrid. Its security was of paramount importance.

At the end of the first school day, Victoria and Romeo went to meet the new pupil and, right, later in the week, David collects a visibly happier Brooklyn.

rooftop was hidden from the road. In a clear sign that David saw his future in Madrid, he took out a three-year lease on the property with an option to buy. The price if he decided to buy – a cool three and a half million pounds.

Despite refusing to confirm which schools they were looking to get Brooklyn into for security reasons, the name of the English-language college the Beckhams ended up selecting was

The Real Madrid boys congratulate David on the announcement of Victoria's pregnancy.

David is all smiles on the news of being a father again. And everyone was keen to congratulate him.

being bandied about in the press almost the minute after David signed his four-year Real Madrid deal. The couple were spotted touring the school facilities with the headmaster during David's first season with the club. But the school reaction to press enquiries into whether the son of a famous footballer was about to enrol was always the same – 'No comment.'

Brooklyn's failure to start school in Madrid that first year gave way to much press speculation that it was because his mum was refusing to settle in Madrid. Victoria would later insist it was because there were no places and she had to put him on a waiting list. But it came as no surprise when Brooklyn appeared at the gates of the college on 13 September 2004 in his uniform of grey trousers, white shirt and navy blue cardigan and blazer, holding his dad's hand for the start of his first day at school in Spain. Part of the reason Posh and Becks settled on La Moraleja was because it was in the area where they wanted to have their eldest son educated. The couple had flown a private tutor over from England to help prepare Brooklyn for full-time learning. But it was a stop-gap solution for a youngster who needed the company of children his own age and an understanding of Spanish if he was ever to integrate in the country where his dad was now earning his money.

Ironically, the shadow of Rebecca Loos hung long over the Beckhams' choice of school for their son. The couple's former aide was an ex-pupil at the college, along with her brother. While David and Victoria are never likely to admit it publicly, she was almost certainly the person who guided them towards their final choice by giving them a glowing recommendation of the school from her time there. And it was the Cuban minders (who the Beckhams were so glad to get out of their lives) who were given the responsibility, while they were still working for the couple, of carrying out a security review of the premises.

At £1,300 a term for pupils Brooklyn's age, the college the Beckhams picked was the most expensive English-language school in Madrid. They pay another £1,000 a year so Brooklyn can have lunch there – a three-course meal which, on his first day, was lentil soup followed by meatballs and fruit. Most British children who attend the college are the sons and daughters of diplomats and executives for multinationals. Brooklyn went into a mixed class of twenty children. The school's 300 pupils – aged five to eighteen – follow the UK curriculum and take GCSEs and A-levels.

The picture of the day was David wiping a tear from his eyes as he dropped Brooklyn off under the close

Doting dad David drops Brooklyn off for his first day at school. There were tears from both son and father.

The news that caused most excitement, though, was the announcement late in the afternoon of 29 August 2004 that Victoria was pregnant with her third child and would give birth in early March. The Beckhams put a statement out confirming the pregnancy around 4pm UK time, about a fortnight after British tabloids first started reporting Victoria was expecting.

'This is fantastic news. We are both absolutely delighted,' they announced.

Significantly, given the number of newspaper reports claiming Victoria hated Spain and wanted David to return to England, they added, 'We are planning to have the baby in Spain.'

It was a public commitment to her husband's career at Real Madrid. The sex of the child wouldn't be revealed in The *Sun* until the following year. But the announcement immediately gave way to speculation about the name. With Brooklyn taking his name from the area of New York where he was conceived, Marrakech was one of the favourite early front runners. Sawbridgeworth, the Hertfordshire town where they have their palatial home Beckingham Palace, was also put up as a possibility. One bizarre report at the time even claimed Victoria was urging her husband to name the unborn child San Miguel after the popular Spanish beer.

eye of his army of bodyguards. The youngster, too, burst into tears as his dad took his rucksack and lifted him in his arms to carry him to his classroom. Victoria took her turn to play the doting parent in the afternoon by going to pick Brooklyn up from school in an eye-catching white Flamenco-style dress under a jean jacket.

Trouble Brewing

Victoria had been noticeable by her absence during her husband's first season with Real Madrid. The number of days she spent in the Spanish capital often barely reached double figures. When she was photographed in Madrid, it was usually shopping in the designer shops along upmarket Serrano Street before or after the home matches she generally attended. It wasn't exactly a positive image for a mother-of-two whose critics said that her place was beside David and that her failure to settle in Madrid was placing huge stress on their relationship. When Rebecca Loos went public with her claims of an affair with Becks, she said David had confided in her that he was incredibly lonely.

But David's second season in Madrid was going to be different. The single man's lifestyle Beckham had led in his first season – the evenings out with unmarried friends and the nights spent alone in an empty house with his wife and kids in another country – would largely become a thing of the past. With Brooklyn now in full-time education in Madrid, Victoria became more of a permanent fixture in the Spanish capital. She remained an outsider in a new city – a woman who the Spanish didn't consider to be very interested in them and who they, in turn, weren't very interested in either. And during the later stages of her pregnancy – amid reports she was engaged in an image-protection exercise and didn't want to be

David plays against Newmansia, and (*opposite*) Victoria watches with guest Simon Fuller, former manager of the Spice Girls. The press were at this time reporting rumours of a trial separation.

photographed looking anything other than wafer-thin – she became a virtual recluse, rarely seen outside the walls of her Madrid mansion or the tinted windows of her chauffeur-driven Range Rover. But Victoria was in Madrid and by the side of her husband.

Critics might claim it was Brand Beckham on full steam and a badly disguised attempt by the former Spice Girl to win the spin battle against those who claimed David and Victoria stood to make more money together than apart. But the fact remained – the

Amidst all the furore in the press, Victoria gets on with her life in Madrid – picking up Brooklyn from school. Her own 'DB' tattoo is visible on her wrist.

More body art
for Becks …

The couple gave up responding to the onslaught of claims about their marriage in the press. Instead, they went for a romantic lunch at the Ritz.

number of days she didn't spend in the Spanish capital were now in single figures, not the number of days she did.

What Posh and Becks hadn't counted on were fresh setbacks – another tabloid examination of their supposed marriage problems and new sex allegations against David. Two days before Brooklyn started at school, the *News of the World* went on the offensive again with a front-page article claiming the Beckhams' marriage was hanging by a thread and the couple were heading for a trial separation. The report said Victoria had branded her husband a 'vain, arrogant yob' in a series of explosive rows. She was, the paper alleged, tired of his growing love of tattoos, which now included a highly visible cross with angel wings on his neck. A source quoted in the paper said, 'Victoria hates his looks, hates the tattoos all over his body and hates the way he swears and rants.'

By now the couple – tired of what they saw as a campaign in certain sections of the media to wreck their happy marriage – were not even bothering to respond to the claims. But it meant all eyes were back on David and

Making her mark – Victoria shows some of her designs to the manager at the Louis Vuitton shop in Madrid.

Victoria that afternoon as they enjoyed a romantic lunch at Madrid's Ritz Hotel. The couple left David's mum, Sandra, to babysit their sons. David donned a dinner jacket for the posh lunch – a near-identical repeat of the previous year's candlelit meal he took Victoria on after pictures of him and Rebecca Loos together in a Madrid bar were published. He hired out the same private dining room he chose on that occasion. And he filled the room with hundreds of pounds worth of flowers before treating Victoria to a three-course meal by top Spanish chef Javier Aldea, washed down with a £150 bottle of champagne.

The new sex allegations against Beckham appeared in the form of a kiss-and-tell by beautician Danielle Heath. In a detailed exposé published in the *Sunday Mirror*, she claimed she had shared oral sex with Becks at his Madrid home just twenty-four hours after he and Victoria announced they were expecting their third child. Danielle, twenty-two, had become a regular visitor to the Beckhams' Hertfordshire mansion, after meeting Victoria in an Essex beauty salon. She would give Victoria waxing treatments and apply spray-on fake tan to her husband and had been invited into their Madrid home for the beauty sessions. David and Victoria issued a furious denial of her claims. And another picture of Danielle emerged in daily papers who picked up

on the story in subsequent days – especially when a friend described her as a woman who enjoyed the company of soccer players.

But whatever the truth behind the revelations, they represented another unflattering portrayal of the private David Beckham that some papers claimed lay behind a carefully crafted public image. They couldn't have come at a worse time either. A fortnight earlier Victoria had given her first in-depth interview to a Spanish journalist. The interview appeared in the newly launched *Gala* magazine, just six days before Danielle's exposé. Victoria had agonised for months about how to turn round the negative image people in Spain had of her. Interviewer Begona Gutierrez had spent weeks trying to get a big name like Posh to agree to talk to coincide with the launch of the upmarket glossy magazine in Spain. After finally acquiescing and meeting Begona in the Beckhams' offices in central Madrid, Victoria gushed she'd like to have five babies and was already thinking of naming her fourth child Luna – Spanish for moon – if it turned out to be a girl.

Questions about her husband's string of alleged infidelities were off limits that day. But Victoria, speaking for the first time since news emerged she was pregnant with her third child, revealed she had cravings for olives and chips with salt and vinegar.

'People in Spain are very friendly and I feel everything is ideal,' she said.

The right to read what *Gala* was going to print before it went out was not something afforded to her a few days later when Danielle had her say. For Victoria, coming so soon after her attempts to win over her Spanish doubters, it was a massive slap in the face.

Above and left: Practising some of his ball skills with two of the children featured in the DVD.

Right: Becks at the launch of his soccer skills DVD *Really Bend it Like Beckham*.

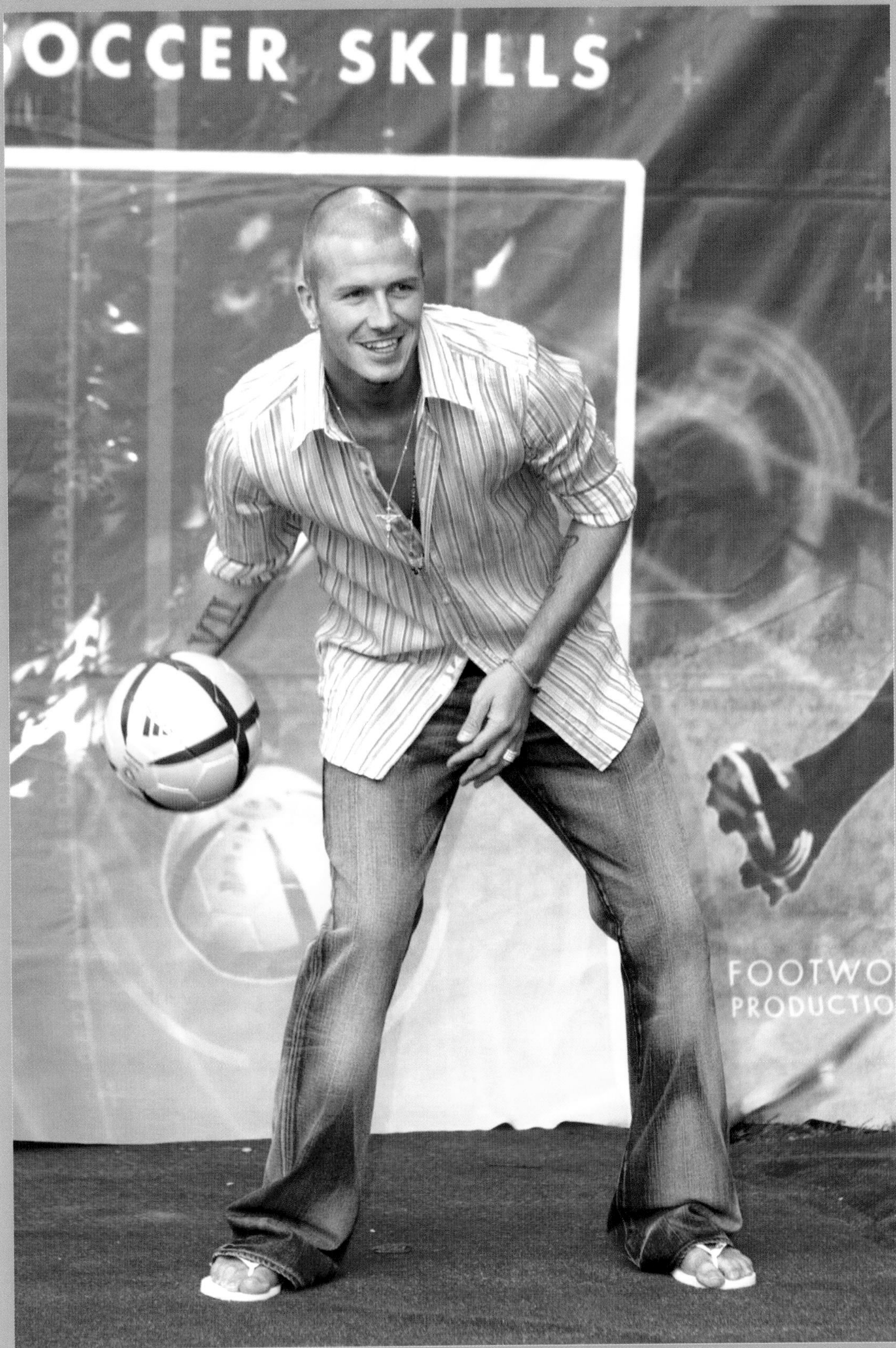
OCCER SKILLS
FOOTWO
PRODUCTIO

Boys night out. Beckham spends quality time with his sons at a tennis tournament in Madrid.

The Home Guard

Victoria's decision to move to Madrid full-time and start Brooklyn at school in the city led to inevitable security headaches. Posh and Becks have always given their family's security top priority. Ever since the *News of the World* claimed to have foiled a kidnap attempt on the family when David was still playing for Manchester United, Victoria and her sons have been shadowed by bodyguards everywhere they go.

Many celebrities – even A-list celebrities – take a more relaxed approach to personal security and try not to let their fame stop them from doing the things they used to do when they were unknown. Posh and Becks, on the other hand, have chosen to share their lives with hired minders.

David drives himself to and from training, but, where Victoria and the children are concerned, there's always security in tow. Just as security was tightened after the UK kidnap scare, so the ring of steel around the Beckhams was strengthened around the family during the summer of 2004.

The couple had been made aware of at least two instances in Madrid of children of the wealthy being kidnapped by organised crime gangs. The Beckhams were advised that the threat to them, as a high-profile couple with young children, was also credible. The exact reason for their concerns was never revealed – but they were taken seriously enough for David's bodyguards to start arming themselves as he started his second

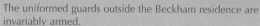
The uniformed guards outside the Beckham residence are invariably armed.

season with Real Madrid. The same was true of the uniformed security guards who were brought in to stand guard inside the gates of the Beckhams' new home. They were supposed to represent the first line of defence against any intrusion on to the Beckhams' property. The top of a gun holster and the weapon inside were clearly visible as one of the guards pulled his jacket back while I was waiting with a photographer for Beckham to emerge one day.

The typical scenario would involve two cars doing the school run every morning – one with Beckham at the wheel and the other with Brooklyn and two minders. Another minder would be waiting inside the school grounds for them to arrive. He would then stay at the school all day until Brooklyn finished his lessons. If Victoria went out shopping it would be with at least two minders. And a family day out would normally involve three cars, two of which would be occupied by the couple's bodyguards, who would make sure no one followed.

With the Cubans out of the picture, a

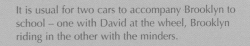

It is usual for two cars to accompany Brooklyn to school – one with David at the wheel, Brooklyn riding in the other with the minders.

There is quite often a minder waiting at the school grounds to meet him when he arrives.

Spanish firm was brought in. The bilingual bodyguards knew Madrid inch by inch and proved invaluable because of their knowledge of the language. They worked alongside the English bodyguards who had been with David and Victoria since day one of their Spanish adventure. The English bodyguards lived, ate and slept at the Beckham household and accompanied Victoria and the children when they jetted back to England.

127

If you were to tot up the hours Brooklyn and Romeo spent with the bodyguards, it would probably come to more than the time they were with their own father. I still remember following Victoria and the children round a shopping centre near Lisbon during Euro 2004 and watching the Beckhams' eldest child playing with one of the English minders. David might earn more in a week than most people can only dream of earning in a year. But the thought that went through my mind at that moment was, 'If this is the price of fame, then I would never want it.'

When it came down to it, though, paparazzi photographers – and not criminals seeking to kidnap the Beckham children – were the ones who came up against the wall of security on a daily basis. Until we are in that situation, none of us can really know how we would react if we were followed everywhere by someone trying to take our picture. Photographers explain it this way – celebrities like Beckham sell, they have a job to do feeding the public's demand for pictures and, once they've got a set of images, they can put their cameras away and go home. David trying to stop them taking pictures is only going to make him and his family a rarer commodity – increasing their market value and enabling them to make more money. If

Although David drives himself to and from training, there is usually a minder at the wheel when Victoria is travelling.

he wanted to stop the merry-go-round, all he'd have to do is let them take pictures every day and people would soon get bored of seeing him in the papers. Why worry about them, waste his time and create extra stress for himself when his home is the safest place in Madrid, with photographers outside who are alert to every movement?

David obviously doesn't see things the same way – especially when it comes to pictures of his children. His lucrative advertising contracts mean he has to protect his image to a certain extent. And if he were to co-operate more with the press, he would be accused in certain quarters of being a publicity seeker. There have been times when he and Victoria have dropped their guard and let themselves be photographed – usually to combat bad publicity – but these are few and far between.

David and Victoria's minders know the photographers who follow Beckham regularly well enough to be on first-name terms. Through the sheer habit of seeing each other every day, they often end up indulging in small talk. But the balance of a relationship where David has the money to contract a private security team and, in one of his high-performance cars, can leave any paparazzo standing means the odds are always going to be stacked against them on those days he doesn't want his picture taken. A typical day for paparazzi photographers usually consists of sitting outside a house they can't see for most of the day – then being blocked in by one of the minders

Victoria and the children are closely guarded wherever they go.

so David and Victoria can slip away without being followed.

As the Beckhams' private life continued to be pored over in the papers, the photographers following him on a day-to-day basis felt the brunt of David's anger. Just as the paparazzi knew the make, model and number plates of the cars the Beckhams used, so the England captain and his bodyguards knew their vehicles. Around the time of the Danielle Heath sex claims against David, photographers would return from lunch to find that their cars had been pelted with eggs. There is no evidence Becks or any of his bodyguards were involved, but it added to the feeling of 'them' and 'us' that was experienced on both sides.

On other occasions David would exercise his middle finger when he saw one of the photographers, who had become his daily shadow, parked outside his house. A paparazzo who doesn't give back as good as he gets and backs down at the first sign of a confrontation is never going to get close to the picture that really matters. But even David, used to the adulation of screaming fans, must have been a bit taken aback when the photographer in question reacted by taking his trousers down... and pulling a moonie.

Brooklyn and Romeo play while David trains... but there is always protection close at hand.

It has been said that the Beckham children spend more time in the company of minders than of their parents… but Dad gets the best job here, helping little Romeo learn how to ride his bike.

The New Arrival

Victoria virtually disappeared in the later stages of her pregnancy. She made promotional appearances in Asia and Los Angeles at the end of October 2004 to launch a new range of clothing she helped design. She returned to Madrid and a date with Tom Cruise – the Hollywood actor combined a visit to Spain to promote his Church of Scientology religion with a trip to the Santiago Bernabeu Stadium with Posh and Becks to watch Real Madrid play. Cruise was invited by Beckham, who was recovering from broken ribs, to join him, Victoria and their sons Brooklyn and Romeo in their VIP box.

But come November sightings of her were much less frequent. When she

wasn't resting at home in Madrid, she would head into an office that she and David used in the centre of the city. On one rare shopping trip to a Madrid department store at the end of November, she looked like she was guarding the crown jewels as she covered up under a poncho to stop her bump from showing.

The *Sun* had reported fairly early on in the pregnancy that scans had showed David and Victoria's third child would be a boy. The couple made it clear from the outset that the new arrival would be born in Spain – despite newspaper reports to the contrary that claimed Victoria would fly back to London to give birth. The Portland Hospital, where

Cruise control – a star-studded night at Real Madrid as the Beckham family entertain Tom Cruise.

she had given birth to Brooklyn and Romeo, was even named.

In Spain, the prestigious Zarzuela Clinic where Beckham had his medical when he first arrived in Madrid was ventured as the most likely venue for the birth. The clinic, owned and run by health firm Sanitas, is a favourite of the Real Madrid players and their wives. Raul's wife, Mamen Sanz, gave birth to second son Hugo there in November 2002. And teammate Guti's wife, Arancha de Benito, picked the hospital to give birth to the couple's second child, Aitor, in January 2002 by Caesarian section.

In the end the Beckhams opted for a hospital with royal connections – the Ruber Internacional where the king of Spain's daughter, Princess Elena, gave birth to her two children. It was also the clinic where former Newcastle defender Jonathan Woodgate had his medical after signing for Real Madrid. The talk before the birth was of Victoria having to fight hospital red tape and

Looking very happy at the prospect of a new addition to the family – and very much in love, as David takes pictures of his wife on his mobile phone.

paying £150,000 to hire out an entire floor to ensure privacy. 25 February 2005 was bandied about in press reports as the date of the birth. In the end the reports about an entire floor being hired turned out to be false – as did the reported date. Victoria was rushed to hospital from her Madrid home early in the morning on Sunday, 20 February and gave birth after a thirty-minute intervention.

A tired-looking David, who attended the birth, took on the job of telling the press the good news just after midday.

He revealed from the hospital steps that the baby had been born at 10.40am local time and weighed just over 7lb. Becks couldn't hide his delight as he told the thirty or so reporters, photographers and TV cameramen who had gathered outside the hospital from mid-morning onwards, 'He's gorgeous, healthy and his mum is very good, so we're a very happy family. He's got Victoria's lips and nose.' But the biggest surprise came when he revealed the name – Cruz.

Bookies William Hill had done a

During the latter stages of her pregnancy, Victoria was rarely seen out and about. The few times she was spotted, she was out shopping or attending a home game. She would often wear a large poncho to conceal her figure.

Above: The Ruber Clinic, where Cruz Beckham was born. Victoria had her own private garden at the hospital (*below*), but the cold snap in Madrid at the time rendered it unused.

The proud new father arrives at the hospital to visit his wife and new baby.

Beckham announces the new arrival to the waiting media.

roaring trade prior to the birth as punters betted on what name the Beckhams would choose. 'Jose' had been 7–1 favourite while other choices included the names of David's Real Madrid teammates such as 'Zinedine' and 'Ronaldo'. There was no sign of 'Cruz' on William Hill's list. It wasn't surprising as the name caught everyone unawares. 'Cruz' is an old-fashioned name with heavy religious overtones that literally means 'Holy Cross bearer'. As I found out when I interviewed Spaniards and south Americans who shared baby Beckham's

name, they very much regarded it as a cross they had had to bear throughout life. Lola Oria, Spanish language tutor at Oxford University, was widely quoted in the papers the following day claiming it was more of a girl's than a boy's name. 'It is quite a strange thing to do to a little boy,' she added.

If the choice of first name was a little different, the middle name was much more familiar. David and Victoria have a habit of giving their children non-traditional first names and more common second names. The eldest,

Brooklyn, has the middle name Joseph and Romeo's second name is James. In Cruz's case, they went for the middle name David – giving the youngster the option of calling himself David Junior when he is older.

Victoria left hospital three days after the birth, on the evening of Wednesday, 23 February. The celebrity mums and dads of most newborns in Spain walk out the front door of their hospital, pose for pictures with their baby and say a few words to the waiting press before heading home. Photographers and reporters covering the arrival of baby Beckham had stood outside the clinic for more than twelve hours a day waiting for that moment to arrive. They were quite obviously upset when the Beckhams' bodyguards put a massive white sheet up so Victoria and baby could leave the hospital without being photographed. The picture appeared in several papers the following day.

Later it emerged that Victoria had given birth in the maternity ward's room number 10 – the same room Princess Elena had after giving birth to her two children. Pictures of the inside of the suite published at the time show a room divided in two by a glass panel and adjoining door. Victoria slept in a no-

The luxury cot that the Beckhams bought for baby Cruz.

Proud grandparents arrive to make a fuss of the new member of the family.

A happy Beckham trains after the birth of Cruz.

frills single bed in one half of the room next to a Holy Cross – appropriate given the name of her new son. David spent the night after Victoria gave birth on a sofa in the other half of the room. The couple's nanny and sons Brooklyn and Romeo were given room number 11 next door. Victoria and her family were also given their own private garden – but because of the cold snap that gripped Madrid that week they didn't use it. Before checking into the Ruber Internacional to give birth, though, Posh ordered a sweep of her room for hidden cameras and microphones. She recovered from her Caesarian with fruit, especially kiwis and strawberries, washed down with mineral water.

Becks spoke about life with his new son the same day Victoria left hospital. The England captain took time out of his domestic duties to launch a new Pepsi ad in Madrid with Jennifer Lopez and Beyoncé. Most of the press questions that day were directed towards David – the two pop stars with him hardly got a look in.

David laughed off the idea that the

Greeting fans who were keen to congratulate him on his news.

David's father Ted watches as his son is put through his paces in training.

new arrival had put him off extending his family. He said, 'Changing nappies is the fun part of having children. It's part of being a father. It's part of being a mother. Changing nappies will not put me off having more. I love children and that's why I have three beautiful boys.'

Speaking for only the second time since Victoria gave birth, he added, 'My wife is very good, she's perfect. The baby is very good as well. He's very healthy, he's sleeping very well and eating very well.'

The Real Madrid boys enjoy
the snow that fell shortly after
Cruz's birth.

Beckham launches a new Pepsi ad with stars Beyoncé and Jennifer Lopez. Despite their A-list status it was David who grabbed the attention as he was given presents for his new son.

As with his other sons, Becks has had a tattoo to mark Cruz's arrival. This one is in the middle of his back. He also sports Cruz's name on his football boot.

Happy Birthday, Becks!

The first family birthday David hosted in Madrid was his son Romeo's. Becks was staying at the Santo Mauro Hotel at the time and organised a small party to mark the youngster's first anniversary. A dozen mostly close relatives, including David's mum Sandra and Victoria's parents, attended the low-key bash. Victoria's thirtieth and David's twenty-ninth birthday were largely lost in the welter of sex claims against the England captain. Victoria spent the eve of her thirtieth birthday apart from husband David in an Alpine ski resort, two days after Sky TV's interview with Rebecca Loos.

David's twenty-ninth birthday party on 2 May 2004 was a far cry from the extravagant celebrations he and his wife

had thrown in the past. Unlike the lavish £350,000 World Cup party two years earlier, bunting and balloons were all that welcomed thirty guests to Beckingham Palace in Hertfordshire. Most of the guests were reportedly dressed casually in tracksuits or jeans and Victoria's family looked gloomy and stony faced. Tennis star Greg Rusedski and his wife Lucy were among the best-known guests.

David's second season in Madrid – his first with Victoria around on a full-time basis – was to be different. The birthdays the family celebrated that year would show they were settling in Madrid – and were starting to put behind them the allegations that had brought so many unwanted headlines.

Victoria hosted a giant wildlife party at the end of August 2004 to celebrate Romeo's second birthday. She held the event at the couple's Hertfordshire mansion and the local Paradise Wildlife Park laid on a children's show. But Madrid was the venue chosen for Brooklyn's sixth birthday on 4 March 2005. It was a children's tea party for only about thirty youngsters. But the mix of children showed that home was now Madrid for David and his family.

Dozens of classmates turned up from his school – brought to the gates of the Beckhams' mansion by their Spanish, English and Dutch parents in top-of-the range Mercs, BMWs and gleaming four-wheel drives. They were joined by the children of his dad's teammates. Real Madrid striker Ronaldo dropped off son Ronny, four, for the two-hour do. Michael Owen's fiancée Louise Bonsall brought along daughter Gemma Rose, two, in the couple's green Jaguar. Luis Figo and Swedish model wife Helene Swedin turned up next with children Daniela, four, and Martina, three. Right-back Michel Salgado also attended with his wife Malula Sanz and children. The Beckhams hired a giant marquee for the

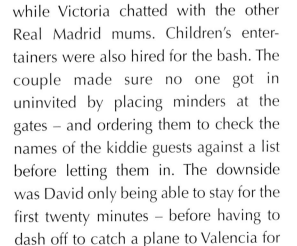

afternoon where the children could play while Victoria chatted with the other Real Madrid mums. Children's entertainers were also hired for the bash. The couple made sure no one got in uninvited by placing minders at the gates – and ordering them to check the names of the kiddie guests against a list before letting them in. The downside was David only being able to stay for the first twenty minutes – before having to dash off to catch a plane to Valencia for a Real Madrid away match.

David missed the day of his wife's thirty-first birthday party because of his footballing commitments. He woke up

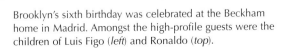

Brooklyn's sixth birthday was celebrated at the Beckham home in Madrid. Amongst the high-profile guests were the children of Luis Figo (*left*) and Ronaldo (*top*).

more than 200 miles away from Posh on her big day after travelling to Valencia with his Real Madrid teammates for a crunch away match. Victoria had to make do with a lunch in Madrid with friends and family, including her mum and dad, Jacqui and Tony.

But David more than made amends during the week when he got back. He left mum Sandra to babysit the children in Madrid and whisked Victoria away to Paris. It all looked as if they'd turned a chapter on the bad times they were experiencing so publicly twelve months earlier. Victoria reportedly burst into tears as she entered the couple's private plane at a Madrid airport to find the seats showered in rose petals. After a champagne breakfast on board, the couple checked in at the exclusive Coco Chanel suite at the Ritz Hotel.

Victoria returned the favour by flying David to the Italian city of Venice for his thirtieth birthday. The couple are thought to have stayed in the Venice apartment of Elton John. But the social event of the year in the Spanish capital was to come with a £250,000 birthday party Victoria organised for David a few days later at a trendy Madrid nightclub called the Buddha Bar. Beckham joked about his age at a post-training press conference a few days before his thirtieth birthday. Laughing as he was asked if he felt over the hill, he said, 'I'm not happy about getting older but at the end of the day it

happens to everyone. My wife is thirty-one so I'll still be her toyboy. I'm looking forward to becoming one year older.'

Asked by one journalist how he felt about being the old man of the England team and the only player in the side who had reached the thirty mark, he fired back, 'Gary Neville's already beat me to it, so you're wrong there.'

The Buddha Bar lies on a busy motorway a short drive from central Madrid. Owned by a DJ-turned-entrepreneur who is currently dating a former Miss Spain, it is one of Beckham's favourite nightspots in Madrid. Victoria spent weeks preparing everything down to the finest detail after making sure the couple's families and closest showbiz friends could attend.

Former Chelsea star Dennis Wise – dressed down in jeans, a brown leather jacket and Timberland boots – was first to arrive with wife Claire by taxi just before 9pm. He was closely followed by ex-teammate Gianluca Vialli, David's parents Ted and Sandra who arrived together in a chauffeur-driven Merc, and Victoria's mum and dad Jacqui and Tony.

Victoria drew gasps of admiration when she arrived wearing a tight-fitting cream top, embroidered skirt and high-heeled strappy sandals. She looked happy and relaxed as she posed for pictures at the entrance to the nightclub in a show of unity with David, who was

The famous Buddha bar in Madrid. *Inset*: Staff ensure that all preparations are carried out to the letter.

The birthday boy arrives for his party. The inset shows the £15,000 diamond-encrusted watch given to him by Victoria for his birthday.

dressed all in black. Both were sporting white diamonds – Victoria a white diamond ring and David a diamond-encrusted £15,000 watch Posh is thought to have bought for his birthday. Showbiz pal Elle Macpherson looked stunning in a pink satin mini-dress and Liz Hurley, who was accompanied by boyfriend Arun Nayar, gorgeous in tight-fitting pink trousers, a low-cut floral top and white diamond earrings. The only noticeable absence was Elton John, who was flying back from the States and was unable to attend. But boyfriend David Furnish made the party. So too did Geri Halliwell, who turned up with a female friend.

The location was the worst-kept secret in Madrid – and a dozen photographers and journalists were already outside three hours before the bash started. That number swelled to nearly fifty by the time the first guests started to arrive – and we found ourselves hemmed in behind barricades feeling as if we were attending a mini-Oscars ceremony. Forty flame-lit bamboo torches had been placed around the car park where guests arrived and were met by car attendants who opened their doors and parked their luxury BMWs, Mercs and four-wheel drives for them.

Minutes before Dennis Wise made his entrance as the first one in, staff brought out two ferns in massive earthenware plant pots that they placed either side of the entrance and sprinkled with rose petals. They also placed scented candles in the plant pots and lit them so the perfume was wafting through the air when the partygoers walked in. Guests reached the free bar through a main entrance with two giant Buddha statues on either side then along a corridor lined with floor candles. A carpet had been rolled out for the guests to walk up – except it was black not red.

Inside, the whole place had been redecorated to the specifications of a Venezuelan designer Posh had hired. (He had come up with five different designs for the evening before Victoria picked the one she was happy with.) The bash started with a champagne reception followed by a five-course Thai meal handpicked by Victoria. The 120 guests ate at circular burgundy tables with white orchids imported from Holland as a centrepiece. Afterwards they were treated to a video Victoria put together of David's best footballing moments, including the penalty David scored against Argentina in the 2002 World Cup. A flamenco group then gave a live performance and sang 'Happy Birthday' as David blew out the candles on a cake Victoria ordered from England with a metre-high chocolate Buddha in the middle. Posh also flew Radio 1's DJ Spoony in from London to provide the music for the disco that rounded off the evening.

Let the good times roll. The guests arrive for the exclusive 30th birthday celebrations. *Above, left to right*: Dennis Wise was amongst the first revellers to make his entrance; Real Madrid Coach Vanderlei Luxemburgo; Geri arrives with a special present for Becks. *Below, left to right*: Victoria's mum Jacqui; Elle Macpherson shows off her famous figure; Liz Hurley and boyfriend Arun Nayar.

The hardened party-goers eventually threw in the towel at 6.30am. *Above, left to right:* Gianluca Vialli; Michael Owen and Louise Bonsall; David Furnish. *Below, left to right:* Teammate Ronaldo; the guest of honour leaves, all smiles; Liz Hurley.

OOH ME 'EAD SON

He celebrates until dawn

HOME AT 2AM
Michael Owen and Louise left early doors

ELT ON HIS EAR
David Furnish was without star lover

DODGIEST DANCER
Liz and Arun hit wrong note as music came on

LUCA WHO'S HERE
Gianluca Vialli and his wife Cathryn

SPICE TO SEE YA
Geri was Posh's only bend pal present

ELLE-O!
Supermodel Macpherson's pal Elle at a showstopper

TWO DO
Posh and Becks arrive at the party

WARNING AFTER THE NIGHT BEFORE...

David and Victoria even paid £2,000 so an ambulance with a defibrillator and a saline drip and two paramedics were on standby outside the venue in case one of the guests had an accident or fell ill. Minders swept the club for hidden bugs and cameras on the eve of the bash. The only hitch came when the thirty candles for David's cake went missing – and had to be hastily replaced with two Ikea candles that were left over from the decorations.

David might have been celebrating his thirtieth but he showed he still had the staying power of a teenager as he carried on until dawn. Victoria partied with him until half-past six in the morning – along with his Real Madrid manager and a handful of his teammates. The birds were singing and the Madrid rush-hour was just about to kick in when they finally left – photographed by just a handful of the photographers who had spent the night outside, tucking into the leftover drinks and food that nightclub staff had kindly brought out to help keep them going. Not surprisingly – with Beckham and the rest of the stragglers, including Ronaldo and Michel Salgado, getting only three hours, sleep – training the following day turned into a washout. Many of the players did just one lap of the pitch before heading back into the changing rooms.

The morning after... the boys turn up for training, looking
slightly worse for wear!

Betrayal

David's mum Sandra was a regular face in Madrid during her son's second season in Spain as she often babysat for them. Another person who was a constant in the children's life was their nanny, Abigail Gibson. Abbie would often appear alongside Victoria when she was photographed watching Real Madrid matches from the VIP stand at the ground. She'd take Brooklyn to school in the mornings, flanked by the Beckhams' bodyguards – then stop off with them for coffee at a nearby Starbucks on the way back home. She carried out her job with discretion and seemed totally at ease with the task of helping to raise two youngsters who, because of their parents, were constantly in the public gaze. If she did

have a social life outside of the walls of the Beckham mansion, it wasn't apparent. Romeo certainly seemed to spend just as much time with his arms round Abbie's neck as he did his mum's.

The revelation that Abbie had quit after a furious row with Victoria therefore came as a major surprise. She handed in her notice at the end of March 2005. Newspaper reports at the time claimed Victoria rang Abbie spitting blood after her sister, Louise, called to say she had spotted her in a London nightclub chatting to Danielle Heath. Victoria knew that Abbie and Danielle, the beautician who told the *Sunday Mirror* she had romped with Becks, were friends. She had already warned her nanny to stay away from her.

David's mother Sandra has been a permanent fixture in the Beckham children's lives.

In the ensuing phone row, a tearful Abbie told Victoria she could no longer work for her. She never returned to Madrid. Her belongings were packed up and dispatched to London. Abbie was the third member of the couple's retinue of staff to quit in a matter of months. The previous year, butler John Giles-Larkin and his wife, Nikki, who worked as the Beckhams' housekeeper, left after a row over their increasing workload.

The fact that Abbie was no longer working for the Beckhams was surprising enough. Her decision to speak to the press was even more stunning. The Beckhams always make their staff sign confidentiality agreements before they start working for them. The children's entertainers hired for Brooklyn's sixth birthday had to agree in writing not to speak to the press about what they saw and heard on the day. Abbie, as a family nanny who had been given the keys to the house and free run of the mansion, was no different.

The Beckhams went to court to try to

Abigail Gibson, the Beckham's former nanny, quit after rows following her night out with beautician Danielle Heath who claimed to have romped with David.

stop her from speaking to the press when they found out she had secured a reported £300,000 deal with the *News of the World* through publicist Max Clifford. The move failed. A high court judge ruled the revelations were in the public interest. It was no wonder Beckham left the Santiago Bernabeu looking like his side had lost that night, instead of celebrating a 2–1 win over rivals Villarreal.

The following day the *News of the World* ran the story over seven pages. In it Abbie blasted Beckham as a serial cheat and backed up the claims of former PA Rebecca Loos and beautician Danielle Heath. The report also alleged the ex-nanny witnessed a series of rows between the celebrity couple and that Victoria had confided in her she was terrified David wanted them to split up. Critics of the marriage seized on the allegations as further evidence that Posh and Becks were a successful and well-marketed commercial brand but a flawed couple. Abbie escaped Britain for a sunshine break the Sunday after her revelations first ran. The girlfriend photographed with her as she sunbathed in upmarket Marbella on the Costa del Sol was none other than Danielle Heath.

Despite Real winning against Villarreal, Beckham's mood was soured by his failure to prevent Abbie Gibson from selling her story to the press.

Real Madrid versus Villarreal.

Beckham arrives for training
amidst the Abbie Gibson furore.

David spoke out against her claims in the press, expressing his amazement and disbelief over the allegations.

Abbie's dispute with the Beckhams is now heading for a second court showdown. As this book went to print, the couple faced being sued for constructive dismissal by their ex-nanny, who is said to be claiming £60,000 in compensation. The Beckhams, in turn, had announced plans to sue Abbie for breach of confidence.

David took the opportunity to have a dig at his ex-employee at a press conference three days after Abigail's public condemnation of him and his marriage first appeared. The press conference took place after a Real Madrid training session. Knowing only sports questions were normally allowed, I had to phrase the question very carefully to make sure I wasn't stopped before I got to the end of my sentence. I didn't name Abbie but made a passing reference to Beckham's own admissions in the past about not being able to trust people and asked whether he felt betrayed in the light of current claims being made against him.

Becks didn't name Abbie either but the answer couldn't have been clearer.

'I find it amazing, quite unbelievable,' he said.

As the Abigail Gibson stories rumbled on, Victoria took her mind off things by going to a Madrid jewellers to choose earrings for David's birthday.

'When you've let someone into your home to look after your children, which are Victoria and my most prized possessions, you begin to trust that person. I can't say too much because of what's going on legally. But what I can say is that I'm managing to keep my mind on football without being distracted by what's happening off the pitch, because my wife and I are happy. We are normal people despite what people might think of us.

'Of course we have arguments like any other couple, but I love my wife. I've been brought up to treat women well and respect them. I know for a fact that, if I didn't respect Victoria, my mum would be the first person to tell me off.'

Victoria used her time that week to search for a birthday present for her husband – and take son Romeo out to lunch in a stunning orange skirt. The picture of her twirling the youngster round in that outfit got into almost every daily British tabloid. More evidence Posh and Becks are adept at managing the press, said their critics. A further sign the couple were happier than ever and Victoria felt more at home in Madrid by the day, countered their fans.

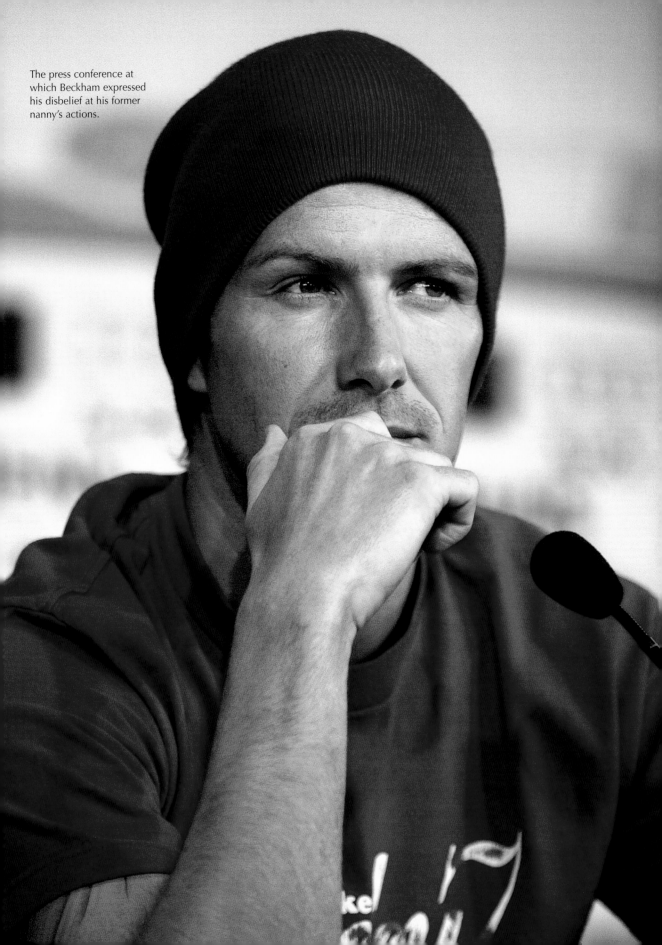

The press conference at which Beckham expressed his disbelief at his former nanny's actions.

looking relaxed and happy with son Romeo outside a restaurant in Madrid.

Casa Beckham

Brooklyn Beckham was now at school in Madrid. Victoria had moved to the Spanish capital to be with her husband and given birth to their third child there. Posh and Becks were still together and – in public – looked happily married and the antithesis of a couple whose marriage was hanging by a thread as alleged former mistresses, staff and some newspapers would have it.

Even David's command of Spanish was beginning to improve. His shout of 'Hala Madrid' as he signed for the club was his only real attempt that first year to get to grips with the language. Come the second year – and despite getting a rap over the knuckles from club bosses over his inability to speak Spanish – he

made progress and started to speak part-sentences in the language.

But as the end of his second season with Real Madrid neared its end, something was still missing from the equation. David and Victoria had a place they could call home in England – their palatial home nicknamed Beckingham Palace. And they had gone a step further towards permanence in Madrid by taking out a long lease on the mansion in La Moraleja where they spent David's second season with his new club. But they hadn't set down proper roots by buying somewhere in the city.

This changed as David returned from a summer 2005 tour of the Far East and

A new home. The stunning villa is the first property that the couple have bought in Spain, a sign that they want to stay.

America. The couple bought Casa Beckham, as Victoria herself admitted she had christened it in May 2005. They moved in at the start of the England captain's third season after their plans to buy the home they had on a long lease failed to materialise. Most British tabloids published aerial shots of the new place and took Victoria's lead to headline their stories with the *Sun* dubbing it 'Casa Beckham' and the *Mirror* 'Casa Becka'.

With David insisting he wants to finish his playing career with Real Madrid, the stunning £4-million mansion is the place he now plans to call home until he hangs up his boots. He and Victoria snapped up the five-bedroom Tuscan-style villa after just one viewing. It is the fourth home Posh and Becks have lived in in Madrid apart from the Santo Mauro Hotel at the start. And it has everything a sports-mad dad with three sons could want. It is also just a short drive from the Beckhams' old house in posh Madrid suburb La

The family become a more permanent fixture in Madrid. Victoria out shopping with Romeo before going to meet the rest of the family at the local tennis club. As always, David found time to give an autograph to a fan.

Moraleja – meaning eldest son Brooklyn, six, could carry on at the same school.

And the icing on the cake as far as Posh and Becks are concerned is that they don't have to worry about noisy neighbours. The land either side of their new home is empty – and likely to be targeted by the Beckhams if they decide they want to enlarge their family and expand their new pad. David and Victoria have previously bought property adjoining their UK mansion Beckingham Palace to stop snoops moving on to their doorstep.

The two-storey yellow ochre villa is reached by a long cobbled driveway lined with silver birches and poplar trees. All five en-suite bedrooms are upstairs. French windows downstairs lead on to an outdoors patio where the couple can eat out on balmy summer evenings. The manicured lawns front and back are built around sculpted Italian fountains, with several decorative ceramic pots laid around the grounds. Its two acres of land also include a tennis court at the back of the house and a ten-metre swimming pool to the side alongside a practice football pitch with a five-a-side goal and children's swings.

Beckham arrives at a
Spanish radio station to
give an interview and
stops to speak to fans.

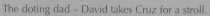
The doting dad – David takes Cruz for a stroll.

Brooklyn, dressed in an England kit, collects balls while David practises his free kicks.

Salad-lover Posh can even pick her own olives from olive trees planted next to the gravel car park where Becks leaves his fleet of luxury cars. Speaking about their new buy in an interview at the end of May, Victoria said, 'We're both really excited about it. I'm really into my interior design and I want to make every room just perfect. I love entertaining and it's a great house for kids. The boys are going to be really happy there.'

The new buy put the final block on months of speculation about David's immediate future in Madrid. The England captain was repeatedly linked with a move to Chelsea and Tottenham as the 2004–05 season moved into its second half. No matter how many times Becks said he was happy at Real Madrid and wanted to stay, someone was always doubting his word. And if it wasn't David, it was Victoria who was

Picking up breakfast and sporting a new look with glasses.

said to have reserved school places for her children back in Britain as part of a planned return.

Posh and Becks spent virtually the whole of summer 2005 away from Spain. With the season at a close, they packed their bags and headed for a break in America, the Caribbean, the UK and the south of France. But Beckham kicked off the 2005–06 season with the white shirt of Real Madrid still on his back. With Casa Beckham to look forward to when his footballing duties finished, David was now starting the third season of a four-year contract. Becks was chosen alongside Raul and Zidane to model his club's new shirts for the season as the players prepared for their pre-season tour of the States and Asia. Old Trafford suddenly seemed a very distant memory.

David always captures attention when he does the school run.

Father and son spend time together at the
Real Madrid training ground.

Galactico

Millions of people around the world idolise David Beckham for who he is and how he earns his money off the pitch, not on it. They are the fans who are interested in reading about him on the front pages, not the back pages of a newspaper. But there is another type of fan who is more concerned with how he plays football, not whether he is or isn't cheating on his wife. The Real Madrid fans who fill the Spanish capital's Santiago Bernabeu every weekend fall into this category.

Beckham sells shirts. He sells more and he sells them faster than anyone else in Real Madrid's history. But when David parts ways with the club, he won't want to be remembered as the player who brought in the most revenue.

He will want to go down in history as a man Real Madrid fans hold dear to their hearts for his football, his passions, his skill, his free kicks and his goals. More than two years have passed since David first put pen to paper on a four-year contract with the Spanish giants and left the Premiership world-beaters where he had grown from a boy to a man. Has he met the test? Has he won the hearts of Real Madrid fans? Will he be remembered as a man who sold shirts and happened to play football? Or will he go down as a man who played football and happened to sell shirts?

Beckham was the fourth big signing in the era of president Florentino Perez after Figo, Zidane and Ronaldo. He was immediately tagged the new 'galactico'

or player from another galaxy – even though he told Real Madrid TV soon after his signing, 'I haven't come here to be a great star. I'm here to be part of a team full of great players, who are stars but above all are excellent players.'

British newspaper editors might have wanted to see pictures of Real Madrid fans dancing in the streets at the news the England captain was joining them. But a big club was used to big names and his arrival was met with muted expectation from seasoned football supporters. Two goals from his first two home games and a string of breathtaking passes immediately won him the hearts of his new side's supporters. He headed a seventy-three-minute goal on his

home debut as Real Madrid beat Mallorca 3–0 and won the pre-season Spanish Supercup on a 4–2 aggregate. He scored again on his home league debut with the new season just three minutes old. Victoria was working and missed Becks kick his first ball in the cauldron of the Santiago Bernabeu. But proud dad Ted, mum Sandra and son Brooklyn flew in from London to see David play.

Critics generally agree that, apart from a handful of decent performances in the first part of the season, Beckham failed to shine in most matches after the winter. The England captain played under four managers in his first two seasons with Real Madrid. All apart from

Beckham's first home game for Real
Madrid, and his first goal.

A concerned-looking Beckham watches a Real match while on a match ban. He insulted a linesman, which resulted in a red card.

Beckham's dead-ball skills and ability to unsettle the world's best defenders with his raking crosses make him naturally suited to the right side of the pitch. And the feeling Becks was being played out of position was proffered as a reason for his failure to convince.

But the off-pitch distractions of the allegations of wife-cheating undoubtedly had an effect on his football. His form dipped after the winter. Some of Beckham's worst performances coincided with the fall-out from the Rebecca Loos allegations. Rather than 'galactico', Beckham's name would more often than not appear in match reports alongside the words *desaparecido en combate* – 'missing in combat'.

Following a 1–1 draw in March 2004 with Racing Santander, whose keeper Ricardo was briefly a former Manchester United teammate, sports daily *Marca* gave a damning verdict on the England skipper's progress in Spain.

'At first, Beckham played football and ran. Then, he ran and played football,' it said.

'After that, he just ran. Yesterday, he didn't play football or run. His best moment was hugging Ricardo.'

Beckham made headlines again at the end of May 2004, but it was for the all the wrong reasons. With Real Madrid in freefall and 2–0 down against lowly placed Murcia after a string of disastrous team performances, Beckham showed

current boss Vanderlei Luxemburgo have played Beckham in central midfield – a novelty for David who made his name with Manchester United on the right side of midfield.

Beckham claimed in a TV interview in February 2004 that the move to central midfield had helped him, not hindered him. He claimed, 'It's helped me a lot. It means I have more of the ball and am involved in games. It has given me a new lease of life here – in Manchester I played on the right, I've been given a new role in the game and it's great to have that. I think I have improved as a player and if I have done that I've succeeded in what I wanted to do.'

Many critics disagree and claim

David Beckham has spoken highly of Real Madrid's manager Vanderlei Luxemburgo. The pair are pictured talking tactics during Real's 3–1 win over Zaragoza.

his nerves by swearing at linesman Ignacio Fidalgo Trapote. The insult was captured on Spanish TV. Becks was clearly seen mouthing the words *'hijo de puta'* – literally 'son of a whore' – at the official. The referee sent David off for showing he had mastered at least the expletives in Spanish.

David Beckham's Euro 2004 was generally considered a disaster and led to calls for him to resign the captaincy. David blamed his poor performances during the tournament on the lax training regime under manager Carlos Queiroz – a claim that obviously didn't go down too well with the Real Madrid hierarchy. Sports headlines at the time screamed things like, 'Skipper's star is on the wane.' The future wasn't looking great for a player who had created so much expectation when he'd signed for Real Madrid.

Beckham has a wonderful track record of bouncing back from the abyss. He was the devil incarnate after getting himself sent off for lashing out at Argentine Diego Simeone in the 1998 World Cup quarter-finals. Three years later he was the saviour who single-

David's teammates congratulate him for his man of the match performance against Barcelona by giving him the bumps.

With former Real teammate Michael Owen, who has since moved to Newcastle FC.

handedly secured England its place in the 2002 World Cup finals with a sensational ninetieth-minute free-kick against Greece.

Beckham has always demonstrated a confidence in his own abilities, which some critics claim borders on arrogance. He refused point-blank to resign the England captaincy – and went a step further by claiming he was offended by the questioning in some quarters of his leadership. Real Madrid failed to win a single medal in Beckham's second season with the club. The campaign was a disaster for players and club chiefs who are used to winning – and whose six-figure spending on players like Beckham has made fans regard second place as a failure.

But critics have seen an improvement in David's form since the arrival of Brazilian Vanderlei Luxemburgo. His replacement of former Spanish coach Jose Antonio Camacho at Christmas 2004 coincided with the return of Beckham to his traditional position on the right side of midfield. Luxemburgo made a dramatic start as Madrid played the remaining six minutes of a league game against Real Sociedad that had been abandoned at 1–1 because of a bomb threat at the Santiago Bernabéu stadium. Those six minutes were enough for Ronaldo to be brought down in the area and for Zinedine Zidane to convert the penalty. Seven straight wins followed and Beckham and the team won back the respect of fans who had begun to question the salaries of some of their supposedly best players.

Luxemburgo was joined by physical trainer Antonio Mello and stunning Brazilian nutritionist Patricia Teixeira. She devised a new eating regime for Beckham and his teammates, which included banning the players from eating chicken skins as part of a fat-reduced diet.

David played an instrumental role in Real's 4–2 victory over arch-rivals Barcelona in March 2005 and was the man of the match in his side's 2–1 comeback victory over Villarreal the following month. Luxemburgo praised Beckham at the end of his first season in

Beckham has won a place in the hearts of Real Madrid fans, and he always finds time for them.

At the opening of his football academy in London.

With the first
academy students.

charge. 'We have this incorrect image spread all over the world that Beckham is only a jersey seller,' he said. 'I thought he was kind of lazy. I was completely wrong. He trains a lot, is very keen to help, a committed player. I have never had the slightest problem with him and I am very proud to have David Beckham in my squad.'

Beckham's improvement in form coincided with a string of reports linking him to a return to London. The *Daily Telegraph* reported Chelsea were prepared to pay between £20 and £25 million for the England captain. Becks was also linked to London rivals Tottenham.

At the same time some tabloid papers were insisting on their front pages that Posh was desperate for a return to the UK – and the Beckhams' Spanish adventure was nearing its end. David responded to the reports by pledging his future to Real Madrid and insisting he wanted to finish his career with the Spanish giants. Speaking in the run-up to his thirtieth birthday he said, 'I am very happy at Real Madrid, better than ever. My life here is great. My wife is happy, my children are happy and my house is wonderful. I've got two years left on my current contract and I want to finish my football career with Real Madrid.

'I've played for Manchester United, which is one of the biggest clubs in the world, I've captained England, which has been a great honour and now I'm playing for Real Madrid, which is another of the biggest clubs in the world. This is where I want to stay till I finish playing.'

Daily Mail sports correspondent Simon Cass, who moved to Madrid soon after Beckham and has charted the England captain's progress at his new club, said, 'Football's big business nowadays and for a club like Real Madrid players like Beckham are the promised land. He's good for the club off the pitch and he's good for it on the pitch. He's already paid for his transfer fee and wages several times over through shirt sales alone. And while he might not be a world-class player, he is a very good player. Ask your average Real Madrid fan and they'll tell you Beckham hasn't got the skills of midfield teammates like Zidane. But he is regarded as a very good buy for the club.

'He's certainly dispelled the misconception I think a lot of Real Madrid fans had about him being a bit of a prima donna who would be worried about messing his hair up. He showed at Manchester United he was prepared to run up and down the park all day and get stuck in. He's continued to do the same at Real Madrid.

'David's got his best ally in Florentino Perez. Beckham has publicly indicated he wants to finish his career with Real Madrid. All the time Perez is around, I think David will stay at the club.'

Life Through a Lens

In today's hi-tech world, a picture of David Beckham can be sitting in the e-mail inboxes of major newspapers around the world less than an hour after it was taken. Paparazzi photographers all work with digital cameras and can download images on to their computers in seconds. Selecting the right photos and cleaning them up on the screen often takes longer than the time it takes to push a button and send them to the USA, Europe, Japan and Australia. An airport picture of Beckham leaving London can be on its way to the printer rolling out the next day's paper by the time he touches down in Madrid. And the public's interest in the England captain means there is no shortage of photographers willing to try and overcome all the obstacles to get his picture.

Magazines and red-top tabloids in Britain pay four-figure sums of money every day for photographs of celebrities taken by paparazzi photographers around the world. Generally, they are freelance photographers working almost as bounty-hunters who give their images to picture agencies and take the lion's share of the sale. The photographers do this because they don't have the time to sell the pictures themselves, they can't speak the language of the countries to which they want to sell the photographs and they invariably lack the sales skill of an agency man. It is no different with pictures of David Beckham.

The *Sun* sent its own photographer to

Madrid for the whole of David's first season with his new club, and part of his second. The exclusive pictures he managed to get saved the newspaper thousands of pounds. However, most of the photos of David and Victoria in Spain that have appeared in other newspapers and magazines around the world (including Britain) are the work of agency photographers and freelance paparazzi. A vast number of those photos have been taken by two Madrid-based photographers who work together, Rolando Cardenoso and Ramon Perez Sanroman. The agency through which they sell their pictures is owned by British Fleet Street photographers Richard Atkins and Mark Beltran. It is called Solarpix and is based on the Costa del Sol. Between them, they are responsible for around eighty per cent of the Beckham output. Ramon and Rolando have dedicated the last three years of their lives to following David and Victoria on a day-to-day basis.

Both of them have been photographers virtually all their working lives. Rolando learned his trade as a fashion photographer's assistant before becoming a cinema photographer, finally making the jump to paparazzo fifteen years ago. Ramon got a taste for the job as a teenager while he was working as a messenger for a Spanish current affairs magazine. One of the magazine's senior photographers took him under his wing

and he has never looked back. He has been working as a paparazzi photographer for more than twenty years.

Following Beckham involves hours of sitting in a car, day after day. Sometimes they can go a fortnight without earning anything. Sometimes they can earn a month's money in a day. Beckham obviously does them no favours! They're not his friends and he invariably orders his bodyguards to try to stop them taking pictures if he sees them. On a very bad day, they might wait outside his house for eight hours – only to be blocked in and stopped from following him by David's bodyguards when he finally emerges from his house. No question, therefore, of an autograph – although both photographers grew up in the Spanish capital and, ironically, are ardent Real Madrid supporters.

David apparently refers to Ramon as the 'gypsy' in private circles. Without naming either photographer, in the string of Spanish newspaper interviews he has given this year he has publicly expressed his dislike of the paparazzi that follow him and his children. It is a tense relationship and one which is destined to remain so. Newspapers and magazines pay good money for pictures of David and Victoria because it helps sell more copies of their publications to a star-hungry public. Photographers would obviously prefer it if fewer obstacles were put in their way. But just as Beckham is not about to turn round and let them take the photos they want, when they want and where they want, so they are not about to put down their cameras. Where there's demand, there's always going to be supply.

'I suspected Beckham would be big but I didn't expect there to be the continuing level of interest there still is in him today,' says Rolando. 'Tabloid magazines in Spain have lost a lot of interest in him. But photos of him still sell very well in Britain. I'm sure David hates us following him everywhere – I'm not sure I'd like it either. The relationship between us is non-existent and, on the rare occasions he acknowledges our presence, it's usually with his middle finger raised.'

Ramon adds, 'I do what I do because it makes me money and because, with Beckham being so popular, I take pride from seeing a picture I have taken appear on the front pages of a newspaper the following day. My pictures sell because there's interest in David Beckham. If I wasn't doing it, someone else would be.'

At the same time as the Rebecca Loos allegations made headlines around the world, pictures of the Beckhams playing in a Madrid park with their children and Carlos the dog were taken by Ramon and Rolando.

'We got a tip that they were going to be eating in a pizza restaurant and followed them from there,' Ramon says.

'I was waiting outside their front door at the time. First they went to a greengrocer's and, from there, to a park near their home. Rebecca Loos was making the headlines at the time and I think that worked in our favour. Things weren't put on a plate for us but we didn't get the frantic car chases or the minders getting in the way as we tried to take pictures that day.

'The Beckhams' lives are played out in the media and the pictures of them playing in the park obviously helped shift the focus back on to them. I can only think that they'd weighed up the advantages and disadvantages of a set of family pictures appearing in the papers and decided it wouldn't do them any harm.

'Rolando and I gave them space and took pictures from about 200 metres away. They saw us but, thankfully, on that occasion decided not to try and stop us.'

Rolando and Ramon also took the pictures of Victoria looking a million dollars in a bright-orange skirt as she twirled son Romeo in the air outside a Madrid restaurant. At the same time, David was once again stressing their marriage was not on the rocks following the decision of former nanny Abigail Gibson to sell intimate details about their private life to a Sunday newspaper.

'Those pictures were the result of a

from another agency and a British tabloid newspaper photographer.

'Victoria's people lost the British guy and the agency photographer. I managed to stick with them until they arrived at the restaurant. The pictures of Victoria wearing that bright-orange skirt and twirling Romeo around in her arms that went around the world in subsequent days were taken between her getting out of the car and her going inside to meet up with family and friends.'

Richard Atkins – who helped to sell the pictures – adds, 'They have been our best-selling Beckham pictures to date and made in excess of £50,000. That obviously makes those photos more memorable than some of the others! But there is also a lot of professional pride riding on them. At least three British papers had sent photographers over to Spain that week and a number of agencies were on the Beckhams' trail because of what was going on with Abbie Gibson.'

Richard and Mark themselves took the pictures of the Beckhams walking along the beach at Fuengirola when they travelled to the Costa del Sol for a weekend break in February 2004.

'I got a call from an eleven-year-old school friend of my son,' Mark explains. 'He'd had a phone call from a friend to say that David and Victoria were eating in a restaurant in a village called Mijas Pueblo in the mountains. I was just

pure and simple follow,' Ramon says. 'Rolando and I were outside the Beckhams' house as normal. The difference that day was that there were more agencies around and a few of the British newpapers had also sent photographers across following Abbie's decison to speak out. Four of us followed when Victoria came out of her house: Rolando and I, a photographer

heading down to the beach for a family picnic and the lad called on the only number he had for us, which was the home number. A few minutes later we'd have left and there would have been no one there to answer the phone. You get a lot of false tips in this line of work and at first I thought this one would turn out to be rubbish. But you can't afford to ignore information and have to check out every tip.

'I dropped everything and raced up to the restaurant which is about twenty minutes away from my home. On the way, I rang Richard to let him know. He was in the middle of collecting his mum from the supermarket and literally had to drive her to Mijas Pueblo and leave her there to find a taxi home, heavy shopping bags and all!

'There were already TV crews and several photographers outside the restaurant when we got there, along with dozens of young fans waiting for autographs. We had to wait about two hours before they came out, and it was obvious from the start that David wasn't too impressed about seeing so much press there. I took a few close-up shots of David and Victoria as they walked towards their car. Richard was waiting at the exit from the village so he could do a follow. We all jumped in our cars and chased after the Beckhams and their bodyguards as they headed out of the village towards the coast. Then David

pulled over and spoke to one of the Spanish photographers about his driving. They ended up losing everyone after that.

'Richard was in a position to see that they hadn't taken the road to Marbella as everyone had expected. I took the Marbella road, knowing that the other photographers would follow me, thereby keeping them off the scent. We took a chance on Fuengirola because it was the nearest resort to Mijas Pueblo and we knew that, with the children around, they were bound to head for the beach.

'Richard covered one half of the town and I covered the other and we just drove around until we spotted the Range Rover and the people carrier they had been using. They were walking along the sea front near the cars. Richard kept the minders busy by taking close-up pictures which they did their best to block by getting in the way. I stood back about a quarter of a mile and took a series of pictures on a long lens. Later, we got some more shots of them on a carousel from a stairwell beside a block of flats. They were completely unaware we were taking the pictures. It was all pretty surreal stuff. I think the public actually thought they were seeing David and Victoria doubles, not the real thing. Getting those pictures exclusively against so much competition gave us a great deal of pride.'

Breaking News

Loved-up
The couple seem happier than ever despite the recent allegations made by Danielle Heath.

Picture perfect
David and Victoria flirted like teenagers on a first date as they watched a match in Madrid

They're so in love, despite everything

The pictures that prove POSH has forgiven BECKS!

ARE THESE THE PICTURES that prove Posh and Becks' turbulent relationship is finally on the mend? After Posh's former friend, beauty therapist Danielle Heath, claimed she romped with David at the Beckhams' Spanish home, friends feared it could have been the final nail in the coffin for their marriage. After all, the couple have been to hell and back in their private life over the past seven months.

The latest accusations understandably left Victoria, who is four months pregnant, devastated, but thankfully it looks as if they have put the recent dramas behind them and the couple seemed happier than ever as they cosied up to each other at a football match in Madrid last Tuesday.

The pair are experts at putting on a good show of unity whenever there are cameras around, but in this particular display of affection they looked relaxed and natural as they watched David's Real Madrid teammates play a Champions League match at the Santiago Bernabeu stadium in the Spanish Capital.

Becks had to sit the game out due to the rib injury he sustained during the recent England vs Wales match, and Posh was more than happy to go along and keep him company. The pair exchanged loving glances and flirted like teenagers on a first date throughout the game, and at one point David even took a picture of his smiling wife of five years on his mobile phone.

After everything they've been through this year, it's good to see Posh and Becks looking content again. But will it continue? ■

30 OCTOBER – 5 NOVEMBER 2004 **heat** 1

Appearing on the following pages are some examples of how our exclusive pictures are reproduced in newspapers and magazines. The range of publications in which they appear proves how popular the Beckhams still are and how much in demand photographs of them are…

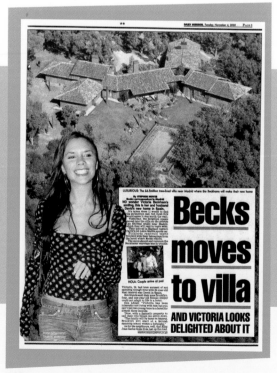

Becks moves to villa
AND VICTORIA LOOKS DELIGHTED ABOUT IT

Beckham boys so happy together as mum and dad aim to prove they are too

He ain't heavy… he's my brother

Tom Cruise loves Posh and Becks!

The Beckhams enter the Hollywood superleague as they schmooze soccer fan Tom Cruise in Madrid, with a view to bagging themselves roles in *Mission: Impossible III*...

With the rough ride she's had lately – both personally and professionally – it's hard to envy Victoria Beckham's position these days. But, taking a look at these pics, we wouldn't have minded being in her shoes last week.

The ex-Spice Girl found herself sandwiched between two A-list hotshots – hubby Becks and movie star Tom Cruise at a football match in Madrid last Sunday. Real Madrid star David, 29, who is recovering from injury, invited Tom to join him, Victoria, 30, and sons Brooklyn, five, and Romeo, two, in the VIP box to watch his side beat Spanish rivals Getafe 2-0. And we don't really blame Becks for gripping his missus' hand tightly with sexy Tom so nearby. Lucky Posh even got a kiss from the actor!

Mission: Impossible star Tom, 42, was in Madrid to promote his latest film *Collateral* and to talk about the Church of Scientology, which has opened its first church in Spain and counts Tom as one of its devout followers. And who knows, after the Beckhams proved responsive to Madonna's Kabbalah cult – wearing the trademark red wristbands after meeting the megastar earlier this year – they may give Tom's quirky faith a try.

The Hollywood heavyweight is certainly a huge fan of David and even told him: "You are my hero." A source close to the Beckhams said: "David and Victoria have met Tom a couple of times for dinner. They get on well. Tom's a huge soccer fan and told David he'd rather have been a famous footballer than an actor. Tom told the Beckhams they can stay at his home in LA whenever they want some privacy there."

According to sources, both Victoria and David are keen to star in *Mission: Impossible III*, which M:I star and producer Tom could certainly help out with. An insider

said: "It would boost audiences in the UK and the Far East. Tom is very shrewd and would be fully aware of the benefits of having Becks in the film."

Life is clearly looking rosy again for Victoria, who is five months pregnant with her third child. A few days earlier she was all smiles at the Rock & Republic fashion show in LA, where she launched V&J Rocks a range of denim jeans, skirts and jackets, which she co-designed for the popular fashion brand. For our exclusive

coverage of the show, turn to LA Stories on page 33.

What's more, Victoria's also in the throes of acquiring a £6 million flat in Chelsea's Eaton Square. The supercouple's spokesperson confirmed they had been house-hunting in London lately, and the flat they are reportedly interested in belongs to Sally Greene, owner of The Old Vic theatre company. She said, "I think they'll absolutely love it. It's so beautiful, with high ceilings, big rooms and gardens."

The Beckhams – who currently rent a mansion in Madrid – already own a £1.5 million holiday home on the Côte d'Azur, as well as Beckingham Palace, their £2.5 million country home in Sawbridgeworth, Hertfordshire. And to augment their property portfolio even further, David is also considering buying a swanky £2 million pad in Majorca, where neighbours include Sir Elton John and Hollywood couple Michael Douglas and Catherine Zeta Jones.

A club insider said: "David is interested in a sanctuary where he can relax before games" – something he'll be keen to do more of after chilling reports last week of a plot to bomb Real Madrid's Bernabéu stadium.

Meanwhile, beautician Danielle Heath, who sold stories of alleged sexual dalliances with Becks while she worked for him as a personal fake tanner, has signed up with a celebrity agent in a bid to become as famous as fellow kiss 'n' tell girl Rebecca Loos. Danielle's close friend Linda Stilwell said: "She's got so many offers, you wouldn't believe. And, yes, one is to promote spray tan. She's seen the way Rebecca Loos has carved a career on the back of Becks and could quite easily do the same."

But with all the glamour of being in Hollywood, it looks like Posh has forgotten all about Dirty Den.

David keeps a firm grip on Posh's hand

Brooklyn couldn't wait for Tom's autograph

> Tom told David he'd rather have been a famous footballer than an actor

Tom's Scientology jokes went down a storm

Look! It's Tom Cruise!

Posh couldn't take her eyes off Tom's white jeans

David and Tom go over the tricky off side rule

David's mum, Sandra

Future movie star, David Beckham

David's son, Brooklyn

David's wife, Victoria

David's number one fan, Tom

David's son, Romeo

The David Beckham Appreciation Society enlists another member

---

DAVID HAS A BOYS' DAY OUT!

Friday 22 October, Madrid

Isn't this just the cutest thing you've ever seen – the three Beckham boys on a day out together? As David, 29, is currently out of action for Real Madrid after breaking a rib, he decided to take a day off from watching the football and instead headed down to the Madrid Open Tennis Championships, taking the lads with him.

Brooklyn, five, and Romeo, two, were dressed in matching denim and looked delighted to be spending some time with Daddy – although the long tennis match did stretch their patience a little!

But the lads managed to amuse themselves with some lollies, while Brooklyn – sporting a shaved head like his devoted dad – made David chuckle.

Despite recent allegations of David's infidelity, he and Victoria, 30, were ecstatic to announce that they're expecting their third son next year, and seem to be back on track after they were spotted laughing and joking at a Real game last week.

We do hope so! Just like Brooklyn and Romeo, we're suckers for a happy ending!

Claire Coleman

BROOKLYN'S LOLLIPOP

Well, that's one way to keep them all quiet!

Brooklyn tells Romeo about how many footballers it takes to change a lightbulb.

The Week in pictures

BECKHAM MOBBED BY SCREAMING FANS

GOING BONKERS!

Monday 15 November, Madrid

The Week in pictures

NOT HAPPY

BECKS' TEARS ON BROOKLYN'S FIRST DAY AT SCHOOL

Monday 13 September, Madrid

SEE DAVID'S REACTION AS HE WALKS AWAY

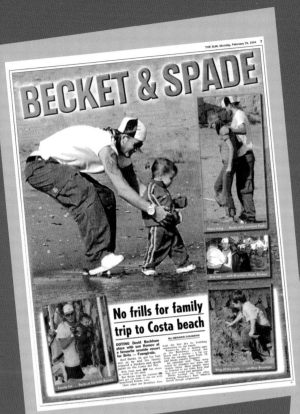

BECKET & SPADE

No frills for family trip to Costa beach

DOTING David Beckham plays with son Romeo at a favourite seaside resort for Brits — Fuengirola.

And Becks, 30, got his feet wet as he and his family enjoyed a buckets and spade jaunt on the Costa del Sol.

With feet cool OFF he stood in the sand.

But Beckham stayed ON and got son Romeo, 21 months, to skip and frolic in the sands with their other son Brooklyn, five.

By GERARD COUZENS

Shore thing... Becks with barefoot Posh

Family fun ... Becks on fun with Romeo

King of the castle ... cowboy Brooklyn

GOOD TIMES

Happy thanks to Cruz

By VICTORIA NEWTON

United front ... couple on Paris birthday trip last week

The wheels haven't come off my marriage ... proud Beckham pushes Cruz's pram in Madrid EXCLUSIVE PICTURE: SOLARPIX.COM

THE Sun
£1.80

PRINTED TODAY IN SPAIN

Thursday, April 28, 2005

Thank ewe my Sun

LAMBS SAVED FROM SLAUGHTER PAGE 15

24-HR GUARD ON ABI

Fears of new attack

POLICE have thrown a 24-hour guard around knife victim Abigail Witchalls amid fears her attacker will target her again.

EXCLUSIVE by JAMIE PYATT, JULIE MOULT and JEROME STARKEY

ORANGE POSH
The Beckhams strike back

PAGES 6 & 7

On me sledge, son

WHAT A HOOT... Victoria looks on

LAUGH A MINUTE AS BECKS AND BROOKLYN FROLIC IN THE SNOW

Pictures: SOLARPIX.COM

A Happy Ending

David and Victoria showed they were a united family and had put any troubles behind them by sharing a tender kiss on a day out with their children as Romeo recovered from a health scare in October 2005. Posh and Becks looked closer than ever – and David ignored onlookers to cuddle youngest son Cruz at an outdoor terrace bar after taking brother Brooklyn to play tennis at a club near their Madrid home.